women on top of the world

*To all the women who spoke to me
for this book, thank you.*

*I believe this is a thank you which
will be echoed by many other
women and men across the world.*

*It isn't an everyday occurrence to
share your intimate secrets with
a stranger, and yet you spoke with
such generosity of spirit, and such
love for womankind.*

*You spoke to redress the centuries
of shame, fear, violence and silence
around female sexuality and to
excitedly share your discoveries
of pleasure and empowerment.*

*You are brave and brilliant,
and I bow before each of you.*

Lucy-Anne x

women on top of the world

WHAT WOMEN THINK ABOUT WHEN THEY'RE HAVING SEX

EDITED BY
LUCY-ANNE HOLMES

WITH ILLUSTRATIONS BY
CHRISSIE HYNDE, JENNY ECLAIR, ALPHACHANNELING
AND MANY MORE

RUNNING PRESS
PHILADELPHIA

*Often during sex,
I would worry if I
was doing something
wrong or if I was doing
anything right, but
there rarely seemed
to be any difference
between the two.*

— MELODIE

MELODIE

- 19 -

UK

Before I started having sex, I used to think it was this wonderful, mind-blowing thing. From what I'd read about in books and heard others say, I thought it would be spectacular. I had no idea how awkward it would actually be.

My ex-boyfriend would almost always be the one to initiate it. I was pretty fine with that. I prefer my partner to be in charge. It usually started out with some light touching around the boobs and, if I was lucky, down around the vulva. If he was feeling adventurous, we'd do it in the shower. Shower sex sounds excellent in theory but, what with slippery surfaces and slippery bodies, it's hard not to fall over – and that's not to mention how you get really cold when you're out of the shower stream!

He'd finger me from all angles, except when I was on my back, which is what I prefer. He could never locate the clitoris. Once, I figured I'd help guide him: I put his fingers on it so he knew where it was. He managed to rub it twice, then slipped off and started rubbing my labia next to it instead. He had no idea he wasn't on my clit anymore. I couldn't stop myself from laughing.

Sometimes it felt like I was being probed rather than pleasured. It was obvious he didn't really know what he was doing and most of the time I was lying there thinking, *God, this is awkward, I wonder when we'll get on with it?* It probably would have been nicer if I could have experienced foreplay where he paid attention to what I did and didn't like. Being jackhammered is never good.

I received oral sex exactly once from him and it was awful. He kept stopping throughout to drink cold water and then go back in. Cold tongues do not feel good at all! I was way too insecure; I wasn't sure which was the appropriate response. The whole thing just felt weird. I gave oral a few times. I do enjoy giving it every now and then, but I have to be in the mood for it to get the proper enjoyment from it, otherwise it just feels like a chore.

He'd always lube up before penetration. The sex itself was okay; sometimes it was painful, particularly during entry. The lube helped. Penetration felt good after all the other stuff.

Once, his mother nearly walked in when we were in the middle of it. He frantically re-dressed to answer the door while I had to hide under the

to them I knew to pee after sex when I finally did start having it at eighteen. And that I knew what a UTI was when I got my first one, so I didn't think I was broken and knew what to do.

We had a safe word, 'red' – we agreed on it when we started having sex, although we never used it. I thought it'd be awkward to discuss something like that, but the conver-

By the time he got the harness tied, he'd lost interest, so I had to sit there and chat awkwardly for a while before he untied me.

blankets and pretend I was cold. It was the middle of summer. There was no way she didn't know, but thankfully she didn't say anything.

I've never had an orgasm, not then, not since. I'm not sure why. Things like masturbation don't do anything for me. I try to tell myself that for some people it just doesn't or that it's because I haven't found the right way yet, but I'm quite insecure about it. I worry that there's something wrong with me.

Growing up I didn't learn very much at all about sex. At around age fourteen I was curious to know what BDSM was, and it was actually from the BDSM community that I learned the most about sex. Reading public forums, I learned about what consent actually is: agreeing enthusiastically rather than just a simple nod or mumbling 'I guess'. I also learned about things like infections and how easily stuff can go wrong; it's thanks

sation was actually very chill and relaxed. We were mostly very vanilla, but he did buy proper bondage rope and once tried to tie a harness. He pulled up a YouTube tutorial and I had to sit there totally naked while he went back and forth between it and me trying to figure out where to put the rope. By the time he got the harness tied, he'd lost interest, so I had to sit there and chat awkwardly for a while before he untied me.

Often during sex, I would worry if I was doing something wrong or if I was doing anything right, but there rarely seemed to be any difference between the two.

Natalie Krim is an artist who lives in California. Her confessional erotic line drawings share her journey of self-love and her fight for women's rights. She likes to use pastel colors and the simplicity of the pencil. ⊙ @nataliejhane

ILLUSTRATION BY NATALIE KRIM

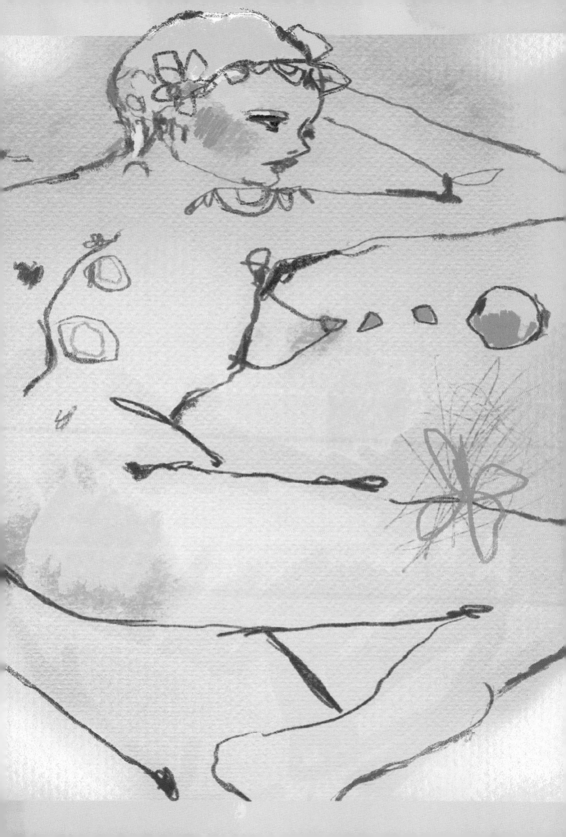

I see numbers and colors when I orgasm.

— WHITE TULIP

WHITE TULIP

– 22 –

JAPAN

The last time I had sex was half a year ago, with a friend with benefits.

We grabbed drinks at an *izakaya*. He said, 'Let's go to my place.' I was like, 'That sounds fun.'

We stared into each other's eyes on his sofa, then he started kissing me. I wanted it to go really slowly, but also really fast, to get to the part when he goes inside.

He took my bra off; it was very exciting. I'm very proud of my boobs.

I said, 'You missed them, right?'

He said, 'Oh yeah, I did.'

I didn't let him touch my breasts. He'd try, and I'd say, 'Uh uh, not yet.' I like to be playful; if he has to work for it, he'll try harder to impress me. In his head, it's clothes off, second base, third base and sex. I'm like, *No! I'm going to mess with you.* It makes it more spontaneous. I like a lot of fore-play – kissing, cuddling, neck kisses, touching, all that fun stuff – it leads to a connection where the two of you become one.

I started to do things I knew he enjoyed: I played with his ears, sucked on them and pinched his nipples. When he reached a peak, he said, 'Please, oh my God, let me do something to you.' I said, 'Okay, you can do what you want now.'

I really enjoyed him playing with my breasts, I have sensitive nipples. I thought, *Holy shit, that feels so good.*

What I hate most is when guys pretend to do what they see on porn. It doesn't feel good at all, so if he starts to go into porn star mode, I say, 'Yo, dude, you need to calm down!' In sex, it's important that you learn what you like, but you're also a teacher to who you're with.

This particular guy taught me about giving blow jobs. Instead of just licking all sorts of places, there's a place, an upside-down heart towards the top of the shaft, that feels really good to him. I make sure I go over that part.

For the longest time, I didn't want anyone to eat me out. Women pee, poop and have periods down there; you hear about yeast infections, discharge, weird smells and tastes. Then

I met someone who said, 'Please, I want to.' I said, 'Go down at your own risk.' It was AMAZING. Now I'm very open: 'If I do you, you do me. Equal opportunity!'

I'd teased him for so long, he teased me too. I like it when the penis is just there and with one thrust could be in you, but they hold off a little longer.

I really enjoy penetration. Your entire body is connected, it's hot

Once at university, I was out clubbing and I met this guy. We went to a Love Hotel. He said I could rest because I had an early start in the morning, but he took advantage of the fact that I was sleeping. It was rape. I got pregnant. I didn't keep the child, because I didn't have the financial stability to do so. I went to a clinic.

Back then I felt it was my fault. I kept thinking that if I hadn't gone to that club, if I hadn't gone there

It sounds cheesy but I want Japanese women to know that it's your life, your body and you're allowed to make your own destiny.

and erotic, but to me there's almost a sense of embarrassment too; it's very personal and exposing.

My favorite position is when I'm on top of a man and we face each other. My breasts are in his face so he can do whatever he wants with them, and our faces aren't too far away so we can kiss too. It gives me a feeling of control.

I see numbers and colors when I orgasm. When I do it by myself, I see a three or a six and cool colors – blue, purple, green, sometimes white. But when it's with a partner, it's more oranges, reds, pinks, and I see a seven or an eight. I think I subconsciously scale the intensity.

When I have sex with this friend, it's a positive experience. But I've had negative ones with other men.

with this man, if I'd woken up and taken control of the situation, then I wouldn't have had to make that decision. But after a lot of thinking, I realized that it wasn't fair, and that I had been the victim, and if I let it haunt me forever then it would mean that my attacker had won. It was then I began to gain control of my sexuality again.

It sounds cheesy but I want Japanese women to know that it's your life, your body and you're allowed to make your own destiny.

MariNaomi is a queer Japanese American cartoonist who makes comics about their love life, friendships, compassion, and the human condition. They are the founder and administrator of the Cartoonists of Color, Queer Cartoonists, and Disabled Cartoonists databases, and cohost of the Ask Bi Grlz podcast. www.MariNaomi.com

ILLUSTRATION BY MARINAOMI

Everything I know about sex is self-taught.

— CAL

CAL

I don't identify as a woman, but I do identify with womanhood.

Sex holds a lot of significance for me, and I'm sure it does for other trans people too. We are sharing our bodies with someone else in such an intimate way. It's an emotional space. It's one of the only spaces where I feel like I am seen as I am.

I like being big spoon, but at first I don't initiate. I think it's a thing for butch women or masculine of-center people; we hold a ridiculous amount of shame, and I don't want to act out toxic masculinity or treat women how I see a lot of men treat women.

There are conversations that have to happen with my lovers. The initial one is:

'I am non-binary, they/them are my pronouns. I don't like you to use feminine words, like beautiful or pretty.'

The first few times I have sex with someone, it will be just with my body as it is. After I have slept with someone three or four times, I start to have conversations about using a strap-on. Lots of queer women use strap-ons, but I do call it a cock and I don't see it as a toy. A lot of the people I have been with have been really hurt by men and I always want to be a safe place for the people I am with – using language like 'cock' or 'let's fuck' might be weird for them.

My favorite cock is glittery with a purple galaxy swirl. It's a rubbery material. It's got a tip to it that's quite large. I wear it harnessed in a pair of pants with a little pocket in the front. If somebody touches my cock when I am wearing it, I feel like I am being touched personally.

I tend to have rougher sex with a hook-up – you're not going to be looking someone intensely in the eyes if you have just met, but my best kind of sex is when I am in love with somebody and we have really, really slow intimate sex – two and a half hours at the very least. I want to turn this person on, show them how much I love them and care for them, without words. Although I do like to look someone in the eyes while I am touching them and tell them that I love them or what I like about that part of their body. And I love it if someone calls me handsome.

I start by doing something quite gentle, like kissing someone's lips. A lot of what we are told of sex is hard it's intense, a real workout.

Everything I know about sex is self-taught. I used to read stuff about sex on Scarleteen and Autostraddle, a queer women's blog. They weren't focused on acts specifically, more

Sometimes they might ask, 'Can you fuck me?'

and fast, but actually once you start to get turned on, the tiniest little sensations on someone's body can be really powerful. I like to kiss people's cheeks, forehead, nose and chin. I want them to feel that every part of them is loved. I even kiss their arms, shoulders, calves – although I am not very good at feet, I don't want to kiss them!

When they are really turned on, it's not just their vagina – everything around that area begins to get sensitive. The key thing I do is I kiss them everywhere except for their clit for a long time. I'll kiss the lips, the sides, the crook where the leg meets the torso. Later, when I finally kiss their clit, I want it to feel like an especially big moment. I should probably be over with the teasing then, but I kiss their thighs again.

Some days, we'll just be having sex and I'll say, 'This feels like it would be good for me, how would you feel?' Sometimes they might ask, 'Can you fuck me?' I might lie on top of them, they might sit on top of me or if I'm wearing my strap-on, I might fuck someone from behind. It grinds against my clit so it feels very nice but

on respect, gentleness, asking about boundaries, what is or what isn't okay and what turns you on. I think this is what teaches you to be good at sex rather than knowing one hundred positions that you could do.

Bárbara Malagoli is a half Italian, half Brazilian illustrator based in London. Her work is all about compositions, shapes, vibrant textures and bold colors. ⓞ @bmalagoli

ILLUSTRATION BY BÁRBARA MALAGOLI

When I have sex, I am trying to disassociate my past trauma from the act, which makes things difficult.

— AUDREY

AUDREY

– 23 –

USA

Sex has always fascinated me. At the beginning, it was like an enigma I felt I wasn't supposed to want to know more about, so of course, I did.

My first brush with sex was when I was about five, when I had an uncomfortable sexual encounter with a peer, something that I only recently started to understand was abuse.

This experience created distrust and fear, which is probably why I have had a very limited number of partners. I realize that when I have sex, I am trying to disassociate my past trauma from the act, which makes things difficult.

I always feel best when I am the one putting the option on the table, then I have an element of control. I can be subtle – playing with someone's hair, or fussing with the hem of their shirt – or I can be blunt: I once called a guy at work and asked him to go into a closet to have phone sex.

I will not have sex in my bed or in my apartment. I'm a writer and work from home, and it's important to me to keep my space private and not create a place associated with memories, as they're rarely good memories when it comes to sex.

I have such a difficult relationship with my body that to allow anyone to touch it is a big deal. There was once a guy who wanted to touch my stomach and it made me feel disgusting because it's the part of my body I like least. The fact that he was bringing attention to it suddenly turned it in my mind into this giant purple elephant watching us, and I couldn't do anything anymore.

I used to be horribly embarrassed about receiving oral sex. Once I had a partner who was mind-blowing at it. It definitely changed my opinion on it. When it's done with communication and consideration, I find myself enjoying it now. It is also because it is one of the few times I am able to let go and get out of my own head. I lose myself, and find myself making noises that surprise me given my personality. I like the feeling of escape.

I have complex feelings about giving. So often a guy will push my head on to his crotch. That is definitely not okay. There are moments where I have enjoyed it because it has given me, again, a sense of control that I really liked; it gave me confidence because I understood how to bring someone pleasure – but if I were told I would never be able to suck a

People who have had really upsetting experiences with sex, particularly from a young age, come to understand it differently from those who had a more traditional trajectory. It's hard to find partners who are sympathetic to that, who give those who are trying to rebuild a relationship

> *My best 'sex' moments have rarely involved it. I find it difficult to relax when someone is shoving themselves inside of me. I can't help but think that it feels like someone trying to put an entire turkey dinner in my vagina.*

dick again I would definitely survive. My last serious partner did not like receiving oral sex because he could not help but find it a little degrading for a woman, and to some extent, I agreed. But there are so few unicorns.

I'm not the biggest fan of penetration. My best 'sex' moments have rarely involved it. I find it difficult to relax when someone is shoving themselves inside of me. I can't help but think that it feels like someone trying to put an entire turkey dinner in my vagina, and once my head has gone to those ridiculous places, I can't come back into the moment.

I would much rather be touched and kissed and sucked for hours. I like it when they're gentle. Don't tug on my hair, don't claw at my ass, don't slap anything. A mouth lightly grazing anywhere near my neck and chest is delightful.

to sex outside of trauma the room to breathe. I think it involves a lot of inner work. Sure, talking does help, but really, the journey to sexual pleasure is something you need to lead for yourself.

Arnelle Woker is an illustrator based in London. She loves to translate the beauty of the female form into curvaceous ladies in the name of body acceptance. ◉ @arnellewoker

ILLUSTRATION BY ARNELLE WOKER

Sometimes my dad pops into my mind when I am having sex.

— SALMA

SALMA

I was afraid of losing my virginity for a long time.

I'm from a traditional Christian village. Before marriage, men could sleep with as many women as they liked, but women had to remain virgins. In some cases in Lebanon, on your wedding night, a man wants to see blood on the sheets, or see it come out of you.

It's sad, I never thought that having sex for the first time could be a beautiful creation between two people.

My first boyfriend was always cheating on me, then I got into another relationship, but he was very abusive. He was jealous all the time; anything could upset him. I had trusted him with a picture of my breasts, something that girls do sometimes. Luckily, he deleted the photo because he said he didn't trust himself not to get in a rage and share it. Instead, he'd bombard me with phone calls telling me I was a whore. We reached a point where one day at school I had to report him. He was

expelled and later he sent me many messages saying if he saw me again he would kill me.

I now work in an organization that helps women who are experiencing domestic violence. My dad was violent towards my mum and I see how that pattern was occurring in my early relationships too.

Sometimes my dad pops into my mind when I am having sex. The first time it happened, I was afraid – I looked into my lover's eyes and saw the face of my dad. It was really painful and scary. Now if it happens, I try to focus on my partner. Sometimes I ask him to stop, and I may share what happened. One partner took that in a bad way but my current partner helps me through it. Our relationship is built on open communication and trust and trying to deconstruct the taboos we learned growing up.

When I am really turned on, I like to belly dance for him. I might wear a long skirt and a bra. Sometimes I don't wear the bra.

I like it when he kisses me on the

neck and says kind words, and for that to lead to him kissing my breasts. Being licked around my nipples and having him suck them really slowly while looking into my eyes. Then con-

with girls. It first happened when I was about eight or nine – a friend and I would kiss each other's nipples and touch each other's private parts. I had many girls in my life I was com-

After sex I will feel calm, or really hungry and want to eat pizza. Sometimes it releases some emotions and I cry. Other times it has left me wondering, an effervescent thought of, 'Do I love this person?'

tinuing to kiss my body until he gets to my vagina and clitoris. I like oral sex; it really turns me on and brings me to a climax point.

We have been exploring me having multiple orgasms; it's something he really wants to encourage in me. I climax with cunnilingus and then he enters me and I come again.

I don't like doggy style very much; it makes me think of porn and I feel like an object. I really like it when we are spooning and he's behind me and we are laying on our sides. I think that is my favorite position. I also like it when he is lying down and I am sitting on him facing his legs, and when we are both sitting, holding each other close.

Sometimes I imagine myself and what I look like, seeing it from the outside. Or I might pretend we are being watched by some attractive men. Sometimes I think of a woman.

I am bisexual. When I was young, I really enjoyed exploring my sexuality

fortable exploring that with. After a few years, I was caught by my mother. I felt shame, but also some part of me didn't feel it was wrong. However, after that I didn't do it again, until a few years ago.

After sex I will feel calm, or really hungry and want to eat pizza. Sometimes it releases some emotions and I cry. Other times it has left me wondering, an effervescent thought of, *Do I love this person?*

Nikki Peck is an artist living and working in Vancouver, BC. Placing the feminine queer gaze at the forefront, Peck examines under what conditions the act of drawing (specifically with graphite and ink) can empower female sexuality in today's society. ◙ @bonercandy69

ILLUSTRATION BY NIKKI PECK

Having two partners enjoy me within twenty-four hours was so beautiful; it's a memory I like to go back to when I masturbate.

— JAYA

JAYA

— 25 —

ECUADOR/AUSTRIA

I had two different perspectives on sexuality when I was growing up. In Ecuador, my parents' lifestyle was very open. My father was an Osho commune, free-love Mexican and my mum an artist. They were often naked around the house and very comfortable with their bodies. In hindsight, I am super grateful for that, although I walked into them having sex far too often for my taste!

Then there was this big fissure when I was thirteen because my parents separated. I moved to Austria and started attending a Catholic school. I had been used to a very tactile culture in South America: you would cuddle friends and say, 'I love you' to them. But in Austria you didn't touch. There was this huge separation between girls and boys in my class; If we accidentally touched someone of the opposite sex then we said we had to get a vaccination afterwards. In sex-ed classes, the girls got taught that if they were in a situation where their boundaries were crossed and they didn't want to do something

sexual, they should not shout for 'help', shouting 'fire' would be a better option to get attention and get out of that situation.

Over the past few years, I feel like an onion who has been peeling off all these layers around sexuality, about what is right and what is wrong and what is real.

I have a very deep and secure relationship with my partner. After two and half years together, I felt the pull of an open relationship. I had been to an event which is strongly inspired by the Burning Man principles and learned about queerness, non-monogamy and consensual sexual self-expression. I was like, *Wow, this offers me the possibility of putting together something that suits me. I don't have to fulfill any standards, wishes or roles that I thought were expected of me.* I was so touched by this revelation, but also scared. I realized that my sexuality was for me to work out. *What do I want?* is one of the most frightening and freeing questions.

One of the things I figured out was that I was attracted to other men and women, and that I wanted to have sexual relationships with them, in a light, playful way, and I didn't want to lie and be with them behind my partner's back. I pushed hard for a second relationship that would run alongside my current one. I thought, *This is what I want and I am going to go for it.*

I have a new lover and I'm in the very slow process of allowing something to develop with him. It's like a

He left and I had the morning to myself. Then my partner came home, and we jumped on each other and had the most wonderful quickie. The contrast of the super tender, sweet soft slow connection I'd had the night before with this rough, fast, strong, penetrative sex – we call it a 'rammeln' in German, like rabbits do it – was amazing. I trust him so I know I can stop at any time if it is too much and he won't be disappointed or angry. We have stopped mid-sex before if

I pushed hard for a second relationship that would run alongside my current one.

beautiful dance, because he comes from a Catholic background and is super shy around sexuality. For me it's never just about the sex, it's much more about the connection.

It was my birthday a few weeks ago. He stayed until the end of my party, until it was just the two of us. We were talking, I asked him to come closer, and it was like we melted into each other. I was burning, ready. He took off my clothes and gave me oral sex, giving space for me to go into my pleasure. I love to visit that image of him going down on me, and me riding that wave and not caring how I looked or how I was.

Then I gave him pleasure with my hands, and he came. We showered and it was the most beautiful shower of two bodies merging into each other. At the beginning of a relationship the union is so powerful and so beautiful. It takes trust to do that.

one of us is uncomfortable and it's so beautiful to know that it won't be hurtful or dramatic if one does so. This was an explosion of orgasms, ripping clothes off on to the floor.

Having two partners enjoy me within twenty-four hours was so beautiful; it's a memory I like to go back to when I masturbate.

So, that's the realm of my sexuality at the moment and I am here just trying to hold my base, in this huge realm of possibilities, of what I want and what I don't want. It's been a crazy journey but right now I am really loving it.

Raised in Liverpool and New York, Candie Payne is a visual artist and designer. Formerly a singer songwriter, she has collaborated with the likes of David Byrne and Mark Ronson. Her first solo exhibition 'The Age of a Flower' was held at RedHouse Originals Gallery, Harrogate in 2019.
@candiepayne_artist

ILLUSTRATION BY CANDIE PAYNE

Generally, I'm scared of penises. I don't mind the penises of men I like, otherwise I don't want to see, touch or hold one.

— VI

VI

— 25 —

INDIA

I'm comfortable with casual sex.

I live in a densely populated city, like most people in India, with my family, so my social space is quite monitored. I haven't had as many sexual experiences as I would like but I've still been able to explore this side of myself.

A life-changing moment for me was when I heard Cardi B on MTV say, 'If a man can't make me come, I will make myself come.' I realized then that I could seek pleasure in sex, and decided that from then on my joy was going to be at the heart of my sexual experience, and pain, unless I wanted it, was not going to feature.

I used to think that pain was just a part of sex. My boyfriend and I had tried penetration a few times before we had full intercourse, but it was agony. On the night we had sex I said, 'No matter how much I tell you it is hurting or how much I tell you to stop, we have to go for it.' I think my partner was traumatized; he felt so bad because I was screaming in pain, but I kept telling him not to stop.

As I got older, pain was always there. Young men are quite clumsy – even those we want to have sex with can end up being violent.

I didn't have words for when I didn't want to have sex. When I was growing up there was this saying, 'You shouldn't leave someone hanging with blue balls.' There was a pressure to satisfy a man even if you didn't want to – if you'd turned him on, it was your responsibility to help him ejaculate.

I also used to feel PTSD from sexual abuse. I was first abused when I was nine years old. I had a string of childhood sexual abuses. A few times it was by strangers, sometimes by people my family and I trusted. Because of my sexual abuse trauma, I only like to date people my age. I am repulsed by and terrified of older men.

I like to initiate; it gives me a greater sense of control. I'd say I've been rejected fifty per cent of the time but I'm always glad that the other person feels comfortable enough to say, 'I don't want to do this' and I can move on. I like to flirt but also be up front. I ask if they have a condom, or when they got tested. If

Recently, I finally told a sexual partner that this happens to me. He was very understanding and afterwards it was better and I stopped

I make it very clear to my partners that I am on a journey right now where I want to feel good in sex, and I am not so much focusing on them.

I am away from home I say, 'Do you want to come back to my room?'

I make it very clear to my partners that I am on a journey right now where I want to feel good in sex, and I am not so much focusing on them. With my last three partners, I had amazing sex. I knew I wanted to orgasm, I led them, told them what felt right, and if it hurt even a bit I said, 'We can't do this position,' or 'This isn't going to work, let's try something else.'

Generally, I'm scared of penises. I don't mind the penises of men I like, otherwise I don't want to see, touch or hold one. I'm more comfortable having sex than giving blow jobs. When I was young, I googled how to give blow jobs, and I read the only way is to enjoy yourself, so if I find I am not enjoying it, then I allow myself to say, 'I can't do this.'

I often dissociate myself from my body during sex, even with someone I really trust. My first partner would always ask, 'Where is your head? I don't know if you are in the moment with me.'

dissociating. I'd always felt bad telling partners that I had a lot of baggage – I thought it was something I had to deal with on my own – but now I understand that we can have better sex if I do.

I like to set rules for myself. One of my rules is that if I have sex with someone, I want to hold hands in public with them for an hour afterwards. The last people I had sex with agreed to this and we held hands very nicely.

Anshika 'Ash' Khullar is an Indian, non-binary transgender illustrator based in Southampton, England. Their art focuses on intersectional feminist narratives, with the aim of showcasing the ordinary as beautiful. ◉ @aorists

ILLUSTRATION BY ANSHIKA 'ASH' KHULLAR

I enjoy having sex with women more than guys – they have more of an emotional connection.

— MARIA LIBRA

MARIA LIBRA

— 26 —

PHILIPPINES

I enjoy having sex with women more than guys – they have more of an emotional connection and they know the places to touch to get the pleasure you want.

I come from the Philippines where talking about sex is very taboo. Now I'm living outside the Philippines in Thailand, I feel more confident discussing it.

I never had a sex talk with my parents. If there were kissing scenes on television, they would switch it off. I studied in a very strict Catholic school with no proper sex education. That is what it's like, where I'm from. Even the word 'condom' has a bad sound to it over there.

I learned about sex through watching porn. I was fifteen, and I needed to know how it happened. I did a simple 'free porn' or 'watch porn online' search and scrolled through what looked good. *Oh, this is what actually happens!* It was uncomfortable for me because I thought looking at porn was really bad. A sin.

I started touching myself while reading fan fiction on the internet. I practised putting my hand there, wondering why people liked it. I didn't know anything about the pleasure of the clitoris. I discovered that when I was with my girlfriend. She helped me explore more of my body.

We live together now. We're naked most of the time. I usually initiate sex but I'm not a direct person, so I show signs by being cuddly and touchy with her, perhaps playing with her boobs. Before my menstruation I tend to feel hornier. Also if I see a sexy picture, or watch shows that have sexy scenes, then I feel like I have to have sex too. Some days I just need affection and love.

I start touching or kissing her sensual places, her boobs or neck – I know that she likes it because she moans. I just think about her pleasure and notice how she reacts.

Then I pleasure her clit with my fingers. I play around the area first, and if I am getting some positive reaction I will directly touch it, make some shapes, go round in circles, flick it. Or I might lick it. I let her be as she moans. I'm focused on the moment. We look at each other; it shows us that we are safe.

At some point, when you touch a clit too much it can get too pleasurable – that's when I start fucking of having sex I suddenly blurt out I want it harder or firmer. She fucks me hard with her fingers. It tends to hurt me, but I cannot stop myself. When I get sexual pleasure I feel I need more and more. I realize afterwards that I hurt myself but it's my own fault.

I like it a bit rough. In the moment of having sex I suddenly blurt out I want it harder or firmer. She fucks me hard with her fingers. It tends to hurt me, but I cannot stop myself.

her with my fingers in an in-and-out motion. I use between one and three fingers; I don't use more than that because I'm scared of hurting her. Or, if that gets tiring, I search around her G-spot, and press on that area a lot.

I know if her moans get louder that she is about to climax. She'll say, 'Don't stop!' If I think she has come, I check if she's okay, or if I am feeling playful I will continue until she comes again. She will have more than one orgasm at a time. I feel a sense of achievement when that happens: *I was able to do that.*

After that she will pleasure me. I am more demonstrative when it is my turn to get pleasure. 'I want you to touch me here and there.' The thing that gives me most pleasure is her going down on me so I ask for that a lot. When she is going down on me I think, *This is what I want.*

I like it a bit rough. In the moment

When I was with a guy, I didn't really experience the highest level of climax that I am experiencing now. When I am having my orgasms now, I don't know how to say it in words, but I am not being held back; it's what I really want, something that can satisfy me. I feel like when I was with guys it was average. But now it's so much better.

Kate Philipson is a freelance graphic illustrator from London. Her illustrations have a strong feminine style with bold lines and colors that burst. She is inspired by popular culture, fashion photography and graphic novels.
@leopardslunch

ILLUSTRATION BY KATE PHILIPSON

I've never thought to ask myself whether I've enjoyed it. Maybe I'll do that next time.

— ROSE

ROSE

— 26 —

USA

Basically, any time I get drunk, I try to pick someone up. I'll go up to a man and start dancing, rubbing my butt against him, which gives him clues about what will happen later.

We'll start making out, kissing and touching. I worry a lot about whether I smell of alcohol or of something I've eaten that day. I worry about whether he is enjoying it. I've made out with a lot of people and yet still I think, *Am I doing this right?*

To me, when you're having a one-night stand, it has to be very vanilla: missionary, maybe doggy. I like to take control, to bite, scratch and spank, but I wouldn't do that with a man I don't know very well so I hold back a little bit.

Usually the clothes come off and I'll give him a blow job. It doesn't turn me on but I'm pretty good at them, I think. I start working my way down, kissing and licking his neck, nipples, sides, belly and inner thighs. Then I suck on his balls. He will get all excited and start moaning. I will put my whole mouth as far as it will go over his penis. I use a lot of spit (men like that a lot), my hands a little bit and my tongue. I'll look at him to check he's enjoying it. Often, I know that this is probably the best blow job he's ever had. *I rock at this. I bet he has never felt this good in his life!* I'll do this until I get bored. It takes about five minutes.

I used to not let men go down on me ever because I have so many worries. I worry if there's an abnormal smell. It's different down there at different times of the month and I don't know what's normal. I don't think we women talk about this much.

I trim my pubic hair, but I don't shave or wax. I've been asked to completely remove my pubic hair before. Men watch porn and expect women to look and act like the women there. When I was younger, I would try to emulate the women in porn, with loud moaning at every thrust for no reason! Now, I'm trying to be confident and not fake anything.

During cunnilingus sometimes I can block these worries out for about five seconds, but then it all comes back.

I wonder about where all these little hang-ups come from. I grew up in the Bible Belt of the States. I never received much information although I don't like it on my face.

I've never had an orgasm with a man in my entire life. I feel I've gotten close, but then gone tense. I've not given up hope; I read that a lot of women don't orgasm during sex.

Many men brag about how long they can last. I'm the opposite of that, thirty seconds would be good.

about sex except that it was bad and something you shouldn't do unless you were married. The only sex education I had was about abstinence. We weren't allowed to leave the classroom until we'd signed a contract saying we wouldn't have sex before we were married. They gave all the girls wristbands which said, 'Worth the wait'.

I enjoy penetration, but it's only fun for a very short amount of time, about five to ten minutes, then I start thinking, *Come on! Things to do!* Many men brag about how long they can last. I'm the opposite of that, thirty seconds would be good. I'll be thinking, *What is the sexiest thing I can do right now so that they will be done as fast as possible with this garbage?* I might breathe in their ear, tighten my Kegel muscles, make some soft moans or whisper, 'Oh baby, it feels so good.' Sometimes I'm just like, *Why don't I flip over?* It must feel really good for them because that's typically how it ends. They might ejaculate on my back, my butt, my boobs; I don't really mind as long as it's over,

Afterwards, I'll feel glad I performed well and it was successful. It makes me feel special to know I was sexy and he wanted me.

I've never thought to ask myself whether I've enjoyed it. Maybe I'll do that next time.

Alice Skinner is a London-based illustrator and visual artist. She creates tongue-in-cheek and digestible images as a social commentary on 21st-century life. @thisisaliceskinner

ILLUSTRATION BY ALICE SKINNER

Working as an escort has opened up a whole new world of things I like.

— GRACE

GRACE

Growing up, I liked the sex worker characters in films and the effect they had on men. Powerful independent female characters who didn't give a shit about the rules.

I used to work as a stripper but working nights became bad for my mental health; you don't finish until eight in the morning. Also, I didn't like the dishonesty of the system, weaseling more and more money out of guys and leaving them with blue balls, dissatisfied.

I now work as an escort, and leave men elated, instead of, 'Oh no, I can't afford one more hour!'

I get a lot of pleasure from pleasing men. It is nice to feel like you can bring someone to a state where they can let go and open up a little. I have always been drawn to people when they are a bit raw; it actually makes me feel quite calm.

Smell for me is the biggest turn-on or -off. Often, I'll see the client through the intercom camera as I let them in; they look young and good-looking, and I think, *Sweet*, but they don't smell nice so it's hard work. But if they smell nice I can get super turned on.

It surprised me how many people come in saying, 'I just want to give *you* a good time.' But it is so subjective: with one guy that might mean I want him to stay very, very close to me and touch me all over, but with someone else it means, 'Don't look at me and take me from behind.'

I have to control the situation. It's not about my experience – it's lucky and it's fun if it gets to be, but the transaction means that as long as it's not hurting me and it's giving the other person pleasure, then I'll do it.

I almost always do oral sex; it's a useful way to get to know the penis before I get penetrated. When the penis goes deep into the back of my mouth, the mouth lubricating feels really nice. But there are certain days when deep throating will be absolutely horrible.

When I'm receiving oral sex, thoughts that I don't want can come into my mind. I might think of a guy

I like, and have to stop myself from coming too quickly, because for the client's sake it has to last long enough for him to feel he's getting his money's worth. Or I might suddenly be thinking of family dinners, and I don't want that! So I wrench myself

not as dramatic or bad as that.

I have never been in a relationship, and since working as a sex worker and quitting drinking, I no longer have casual sex. It was usually not much better, if not worse, than sex I got paid for so I'd wake up the

More than anything I have a deep desire to meet someone who I can connect with on a physical and emotional level.

out of there. Also, it can feel a bit confusing getting nice sensations from someone you are distinctly not attracted to or feel negativity towards.

Penetration is normally the best and easiest moment. I can relax; it doesn't feel like I have to do much. To be entered is enough in some ways. I can be turned on by the sensation of it, regardless of the smell, the look or the feel of the person.

I love being penetrated when I'm on my belly with my legs together, doggy style. When I was younger I used to like being on top because it was how I could orgasm, now I get frustrated with how quickly I come. If I have one of those riding-on-top orgasms I won't be able to have one of those deep, full orgasms later. I'll have blown it on a cheap deal.

Working as an escort has opened up a whole new world of things I like. I wouldn't have asked someone to lick my arsehole but then a client does and it feels quite nice. But other things have taught me to . . . I was going to say grin and bear it, but it's

next morning thinking, *I didn't make any money and I didn't fall in love, what's the point?*

More than anything I have a deep desire to meet someone who I can connect with on a physical and emotional level. I am incredibly comfortable being naked and physical with people I barely know and who barely know me. But actually what feels erotic, exciting, scary, new and vulnerable is being with someone who actually knows me. That turns out to be a much harder thing to find.

Regards Coupables is an illustrator, graphic designer, musician and videographer based in Paris. Through his simple, clean-line illustrations, he likes to express a sense of tongue-in-cheek sexuality that gets right to the point.
🔘 @regards_coupables

ILLUSTRATION BY REGARDS COUPABLES

You need to be able to talk about sex freely, but it is a very sensitive subject. Guys can either find it sexy if you are confident in this area, or they can call you bitch or whore or slut.

— EMILY

EMILY

— 27 —

AUSTRALIA

I've been with my partner for almost six years. We live together, and it's wonderful. Recently, the sex has been a little more adventurous, which is exciting.

Having sex is really important – if we're not really enjoying it, we need to have those 'What should we do?' chats. Tastes definitely change, or you get bored. Then you need to spice things up, otherwise you stop wanting to have sex, which can affect your physical and emotional relationship.

My partner and I have got quite a few sex toys lately, which has been quite fun. In the beginning, they were mainly used on me. Now I can use some of them on him. I definitely love a vibrating cock ring, I really do, it feels so nice on the clitoris. I like handcuffs and blindfolds. A butt plug here and there is okay.

Role play has to be a bit more organized. We have to warn each other and get prepared. We are both a bit control-freaky and nerdy. We love *Star Trek*, *Star Wars* and fantasy and we have a couple of costumes each. I become Lieutenant Nyota Uhura in one of the original teeny tiny costumes.

There is a James Bond role play where he saves me. He wears a suit, I'll bouffe up my hair and wear a little dress. He lathers on the British accent I try to do a Russian accent – 'Thank you for saving me, is there anything I can do' – but I butcher it every time, and he laughs at me.

I like lots of little, soft, cheeky kisses up my neck and up my ear, although if there is too much breathing in my ear early on, it puts me off and reduces my happiness on the inside. It's too stimulating at that point, but later on I love it. We start making out, not too fast or aggressive. There's a little bit of face touching and hair grabbing, but gentle or that does not help me in any way.

We will look in each other's eyes to quickly assess who will go down on who first. We are getting a bit older now – sometimes his back will hurt, so I will go down on him, or my neck will ache, so he will go down on me.

If we are in the kitchen, neither of us will get on the hard floor with our knees anymore, which is quite funny.

I start kissing him around his neck and then I will go slowly down. It depends on how much I really want

He means well and he tries so hard, and I love him so much.

You need to be able to talk about sex freely, but it is a very sensitive subject. Guys can either find it sexy if you are confident in this area, or they

It's nice to feel powerful in the bedroom. I'm fascinated by that relationship between power and enjoyment.

to tease him. Generally, I kiss the area around his thighs, and then his balls, and then up his penis and then down his penis. If I'm feeling particularly provocative, I leave his penis and go back to the areas around it. There is something powerful about watching them react in the way that you want – if you touch here or touch there and they freak out, it's really quite fun. It's nice to feel powerful in the bedroom. I'm fascinated by that relationship between power and enjoyment.

I enjoy giving it more. I do like him going down on me, but I would rather sixty-nine than him spending a lot of time down there. He can get a little bit carried away sometimes – he gets too excited and misses the area. Occasionally, if everything's okay with him at work, I can totally tell him. He's got a big wonderful ego, it can take a lot of knocks, but if he's worried about his masculinity then it will feel more of a personal attack. What goes on in the immediate world can affect us. When he pointed this out to me, I was like, 'Okay, fair enough, babe, I'm sorry.' I'm a psychologist, so I get it.

can call you bitch or whore or slut. Some of my exes were very uncomfortable talking about sex, which is why they are no longer part of my life.

Elsa Rose Frere is an illustrator based in Bath, England. Mainly working in a mixture of gouache paint, colored pencil and digital editing, she uses a textured hand-drawn approach to all of her subjects. ◉ @elsarosefrere

ILLUSTRATION BY ELSA ROSE FRERE

We might be at the height of arousal and I will almost grit my teeth with rage and tell her how much I love her … Sometimes I almost hurt her, I can't help myself.

— ALESSANDRA

ALESSANDRA

– 28 –

ITALY

My partner and I have been together for years. Maybe it's because I'm thinking about our future together, but lately, I've been fantasising about her being pregnant. I literally think, *I just want to impregnate you* even though it is anatomically impossible for me and her. I'll focus on her body, imagining what she would look like with a pregnant belly, the way her skin will stretch and her breasts will swell, and it will turn me on.

I'm very much in love with her. I get moved just thinking about it. I get excited by the way that she talks and how kind she is. Kindness is the sexiest quality. I am very attracted to her.

I might be watching her doing the dishes, working on her laptop or reading a book, and I'll want to go over to her and kiss her. I've always naturally been the initiator; I feel empowered by that. My thoughts are quite playful – *I wonder if she will be up for it if . . . ? I wonder if she will be mad if . . . ?* – knowing that the worst that can happen is she'll tell me to bugger off. There is implicit trust between us that I am not trying to violate anything.

I'll start kissing and touching her, and I'll take it slowly just to make sure she is one hundred per cent up for it. I never rush it. I will run my hands down over her chest and waist. I see how she reacts step by step, listening for audio clues before I progress – the way her breathing changes, for specific sighs.

Usually just when she is almost naked, she asks me to take my clothes off. I find that really arousing. That's an incredible feeling, a sense of validation that she wants to see and enjoy my naked body.

I could spend the entire sexual act just looking at her lips. She is very vocal – 'Can you do that more?' or 'I like what you're doing'. I think it's really cool that she trusts me enough to verbalize what pleases her, without shame, fear or reservation.

I like to be on top of her watching her body move and convulse underneath me, looking at her breasts. I do a rocking movement that mimics the movement of heterosexual sex when a man is penetrating a woman. There is a power in this; I visualize myself with a penis, thinking I would like to place my genes inside of her body.

She is a female ejaculator and I make sure it happens every time. It is nice for me to have visual proof that she enjoyed herself. This used to be

We might be at the height of arousal and I will almost grit my teeth with rage and tell her how much I love her. *Oh my goodness, this person is mine and I love her and I want to have her.* It translates into me physically holding on to her, tightening my grip as I think this. Sometimes I almost hurt her, I can't help myself.

Lesbian porn content is so abysmal that when I masturbate I watch heterosexual porn . . . I wonder whether those images of the man penetrating the woman and the woman enjoying it have projected themselves on to me having sex with my partner.

almost embarrassing for her. I'm glad that I have been able to work through it with her. I love watching what happens to her body when she climaxes.

I don't care if I climax or not, but I do every time. It happens when she has just come and I feel the release in her body. Then I feel ready to orgasm myself. It could be with her stimulating me or with me physically on top of her, my clitoris resting on hers.

Lesbian porn content is so abysmal that when I masturbate I watch heterosexual porn. It's just as bad, however it appears more natural and less staged. I wonder whether those images of the man penetrating the woman and the woman enjoying it have projected themselves on to me having sex with my partner.

Sabrina Gevaerd is a Brazilian illustrator based in London. She likes to explore the intersection between life and magic, with elements that range from female features to animals.
@sabrinagevaerd

I'VE NEVE

ORGASM,

NOT S

— MELODIE

R HAD AN

NOT THEN,

INCE.

This is really new for me and even three years into the relationship, I am getting used to this notion of 'making love' rather than 'having sex'.

— LISA

LISA

— 29 —

AUSTRIA

I'm in a relationship with an Italian guy. For him, it's not about having sex, it's about a real desire to be very close to the person you love. This is really new for me and even three years into the relationship, I am getting used to this notion of 'making love' rather than 'having sex'.

In the past, I've always been very focused on pleasing men, not thinking about me. I think it came from a stupid remark I heard when I was a teenager — somebody said, 'If you don't have good sex, the relationship is over.' It's been drummed into me that in order to keep a man I needed to perform well. Also, I have been with many men who have watched too much porn, and I used to go ahead with what I thought they liked to do, rather than saying to them, 'If you do that again, I think I might throw up.'

Men think that it's a good idea to put their hands on your head when you are giving a blow job and push you down because every porn movie shows that. The number of times I gagged thinking I would throw up any

second, tears rolling down my face. But I'd carry on because I thought that was what gave them pleasure. Even if we had sex after that, there was no fucking way I would come because I was so disturbed by what had happened.

It was very surprising to me that my Italian boyfriend didn't do that. I remember the first time I gave him a blow job; he didn't come the same way as everyone else had. I thought I was doing it wrong. But he said, 'No, I want to see you, to make eye contact. This is you doing this for me. I want to touch you and see you. It isn't a mechanical going up and down.' I am almost a little insecure now because it's not me being an object, I have to find who I am in sex – I was putting on an act before.

I will initiate sex. I'll go towards him, sit on his lap and whisper some fantasy in his ear. I'll simply get undressed in front of him, or I will get out of the bathroom and let my towel drop. But then I want him to take charge. If he doesn't, or if he's not in the mood, I feel rejected. There's a voice inside me asking, *What did I do wrong? Am I good enough in bed? Am I not alluring enough?*

I am a little bit reserved when he goes down on me. I don't want to put him in a situation he might not like, and I'm very concerned about the time it might take me to come. I worry that he thinks I'm not enjoying it.

I had one boyfriend who never went down on me. He said he tried

woman's head. I don't think a man would ever think like that. The amount of time women don't come, and I don't think men worry, *Maybe I should shave my chest next time or do more workouts?* It's always the women who think, *Oh my God, the fault is mine.*

> *I'm a perfectionist. I need to perform perfectly. If we had sex and he didn't come, it would be disastrous for me, 'What did I do wrong? Didn't I shave enough? Should I lose two more kilos to be more attractive?'*

it once and didn't like it. Can you imagine if a woman said that about giving blow jobs?

I think a lot during sex. I'm still mostly worried about whether I am doing it right and whether I am pleasing my partner. I do think about whether I am enjoying it too, but less so. I don't tend to lose myself in the moment; I'm not sure anyone really does. All this thinking sometimes prevents me from coming at all.

I'm a perfectionist. I need to perform perfectly. If we had sex and he didn't come, it would be disastrous for me. *What did I do wrong? Didn't I shave enough? Should I lose two more kilos to be more attractive?*

These thoughts shouldn't be in a

Mattia Cavanna is an Italian engineer living in Washington, D.C. He is an award-winning painter in his spare time, specializing in oil painting.
@mattia_17771

ILLUSTRATION BY MATTIA CAVANNA

For five or six years, I suspected I had a medical condition which meant I wasn't capable of orgasm. Then at twenty-four, I made a conscious decision to explore this part of me because it felt like I had a hand and wasn't using it.

— OLGA

OLGA

— 29 —

RUSSIA

I learned about sex from the film *Titanic*, the scene where they are in storage. I was eight years old thinking, *Oh, this what everything is about!* Sex education in Russia was non-existent and my mother had me later in life, so there was a big generational gap. She didn't want to talk about sex or boyfriends, so I had to figure it all out for myself. I lost my virginity at nineteen; it was all very scary for me.

For five or six years, I suspected I had a medical condition which meant I wasn't capable of orgasm. Then at twenty-four, I made a conscious decision to explore this part of me because it felt like I had a hand and wasn't using it.

I bought some books. One of them was written by Samantha from *Sex and the City*. She was in her forties and hadn't had much fun having sex up to that point. I thought, *Oh my God, if a woman like that is having problems in the bedroom, then it's fine to question your sexuality.* It helps when you hear other women's stories, and you realize that there is absolutely no wrong or right.

I'm very into talking. We need to lie naked in bed talking first. Our faces are right up close to each other. Normally after about half an hour we fall silent and start kissing. I love kissing. If it were up to me, I'd spend more time kissing. I don't like too much tongue, but I really like it when we bite each other's lips.

My last boyfriend would go down on me, but he didn't like the favor back, he said it was 'too tender'. I was like, *Oh my God, I've found the perfect man.* It was awkward for me when he first went down on me. *Why am I taking so long?* Sometimes completely irrelevant thoughts popped in my head: *Did I send that email?*

After four weeks I said, 'I am going to say some things about sex.' I told him I worry I'm taking too long and that I don't always come when I have sex. For me to say these things was unprecedented. I remember shaking, my voice trembling, but it was probably the bravest thing I've done in my personal life. I am so glad I did it because he told me about this weird sexual thing that he had going on too. He really likes his balls squeezed really hard; if you squeeze hard enough he can come and that's not something I would have figured out for myself! It was an amazing exchange.

Most of the time I climax with cunnilingus. I like a lot of circular is good in a relationship, what do you do to make it more exciting? I start thinking about ways to spice things up . . . role play, or different places we can have sex in, like caves, and fields, and beaches.

I like lying there on top, my head on his chest, for a long time after, with him still being inside. That's almost

> *I like lying there on top, my head on his chest, for a long time after, with him still being inside. There is nothing else coming to surprise you, nothing else you are waiting for, just the calm and quietness.*

motion around my clitoris and a finger inside. I'll pinch my nipples. This is something I learned through a partner who liked BDSM. He'd put clamps on my nipples. It freaked me out at first but it feels good, then when they're taken off it feels a different sort of good.

From cunnilingus I'll pull him up to kiss and have penetrative sex. I like being on top, I can control my climax more. It really makes me feel sexy to assume this power. I see the whole thing from the outside. I can see him and me, with my long hair, a woman capable of having pleasure.

I'll be moving and leaning on him, touching his chest or reaching behind and clutching his balls. Sometimes I have a weird thought; it's hard to formulate . . . *Is this it? Is there more?* When you get to the point when sex

the best part for me, like the morning after Christmas – you've opened all the presents, the mess, fuss and loud dinner is over, and you're just there enjoying the moment. There is nothing else coming to surprise you, nothing else you are waiting for, just the calm and quietness.

Bárbara Malagoli is a half Italian, half Brazilian illustrator based in London. Her work is all about compositions, shapes, vibrant textures and bold colors. ◉ @bmalagoli

ILLUSTRATION BY BÁRBARA MALAGOLI

I wonder whether it is racist to have sexual preferences for certain races. I think it is – attraction stems from somewhere, it doesn't exist in a bubble.

— ELISIA

ELISIA

I've not had a relationship since I was twenty-six.

I have tried to do one-night stands but it repulses me to engage sexually with someone I don't know. On three different occasions I've found myself running out of hotel rooms.

I am very touch-starved now. I'm physical with my friends – I'll play with their hair, hug them and stroke their skin. Sometimes I get a, 'Ooh, you're so touchy, Elisia,' and all I did was squeeze their arm. Being tactile is almost taboo; I think I get away with it because I'm a girl.

Typically, I masturbate every other night. I use coconut oil and my hands. I don't usually use any additional stimuli although there used to be an ASMR Tumblr I liked. ASMR is a trend where you listen to certain sounds or people speaking softly and enjoy the pleasant tingling feelings you get. This Tumblr had British guys and girls posting audio clips. I liked it when the things said were from relationships, like a guy saying, 'Hey babe, are you home?'

I come up with a whole fantasy scenario. These are always geared towards being in a relationship where I really know my partner, who, depending on my mood, could be a man or a woman or someone who is intersex.

I recognise my sexuality as pansexual or demisexual. I can be attracted to someone regardless of whether they are a male or a female, trans, hermaphrodite, or intersex. It doesn't matter to me as long as I am connected to the personality.

I imagine that this person is in a hotel room and I visit them. Immediately it is very complimentary with non-stop physical contact. He or she would hug me, play with my hair; we sit on each other's laps. It's gentle and connected, but always with an urgency, like, 'It's been so long, I have really been missing your touch,' I think because it has been so long for me.

I've put on quite a bit of weight in the last couple months and things become a bit more complicated if I have my eyes open, which is so bad because we are in the age of feminism! Sometimes my belly gets in the way or my hand brushes my thigh and I think, *Urgh, it's so soft!* When this happens, I play up the compliments in my fantasy even more or

tionship developed a power dynamic – there was power there for me in that the white boy wanted me. I was colonizing the colonizer; when he wanted me I felt I was winning.

It was a small town and very cliquish. There was an Asian table in my

I have a bit of an oral fixation; sometimes I'll bite my lips or put my hand in my mouth.

have my partner focus on that part with love. In my mind, he might bite on my tummy a little or scratch my thigh.

I have a bit of an oral fixation; sometimes I'll bite my lips or put my hand in my mouth. My mouth gets hypersensitive when I am nearing climax. Running my tongue along my teeth doesn't feel like my mouth, it feels like someone else's mouth or someone else's body. Running my tongue along my cheek can nearly tip me over.

I'm usually able to orgasm before the fantasy even progresses to full intercourse or before him or her coming. For me, orgasm is a sharpening of all my senses and a release of all my muscles, like a warm bath.

Occasionally, maybe only ten per cent of the time, I will pleasure the other person in my fantasy, but when that happens, they need to beg me.

I went to university overseas. I saw a guy for a year and a half; he didn't want to commit properly but I lost my virginity to him. This rela-

dormitory and that was where the Asian kids sat. People said to me, 'Oh, you're a new joining Asian kid.' Never in my life had I been identified as an Asian kid. Asia is like fucking huge!

My friends and I suffered a couple of racist attacks when we were out and about, nothing overtly physical, but it was still throwing eggs and dirty dishwater. When I was having sex with my partner, I would remember this and think, *Yeah, yeah, fuck you*, which is so bad.

I wonder whether it is racist to have sexual preferences for certain races. I think it is – attraction stems from somewhere, it doesn't exist in a bubble.

Tina Maria Elena Bak is a French Danish artist living in Denmark. Her specialization is sensual and erotic art from a woman's perspective, using watercolors. ◎ @tinamariaelena

ILLUSTRATION BY TINA MARIA ELENA BAK

I struggled with my body image; I didn't feel woman enough or human enough. I had decided that I couldn't tell anyone I had been cut and that marriage wasn't for me. I don't remember being mad; it was more an apathetic acceptance of fate which I felt in other areas too: 'Me and my life, in many ways, are doomed.'

— WAMBUI

WAMBUI

— 32 —

KENYA

FGM affects your entire life. It cripples you, makes you feel less of a human.

I got cut in 2000 as a rite of passage. 'You no longer have a clitoris, now you are a woman.' But there was no advice; no one spoke to me about it. Even now, I've never even heard the word sex said by any member of my family.

When I was seventeen, someone close to me used to harass me sexually. He'd pull my trousers down, show me his finger and wave it around saying he was going to put it in me. I didn't even know anything about fingering. He didn't rape me, but he'd put his hand in my panties and threaten me. The year I turned eighteen, I got so stressed I attempted suicide.

I struggled with my body image; I didn't feel woman enough or human enough. I had decided that I couldn't tell anyone I had been cut and that marriage wasn't for me. I don't remember being mad; it was more an apathetic acceptance of fate which I

felt in other areas too: *Me and my life, in many ways, are doomed.*

Eventually I met someone, and we did get married. Sexually he was gentle and tried to make me comfortable, but even so I really struggled. He knew I didn't feel woman enough. He'd say, 'I just want you to lie on the bed, I want to look at you,' but I could never do that. I hated my legs being apart and having someone looking at me, because the first time that happened I was cut. I couldn't have sex during the day, only in darkness under the sheets. I didn't want to look at my own body, let alone let someone else see it.

We would have penetrative sex, but I wouldn't be wet and his body would rub against the scar tissue. I'd hold my jaw tight waiting for it to end. Three months after we got married, he died in a car crash. One of the thoughts I had was, *Phew, at least I don't have to have sex anymore,* and that broke my heart.

Afterwards I decided to take stock. I was only twenty-eight. I knew

I had psychological trauma, so I started to look for counselling, but I also knew that what had been taken away from me physically was an seeing how enthusiastically he gives it to me, I can tell he just wants me to be happy. Because I enjoy it so much I try not to come too quickly; the more

I underwent restorative surgery . . . It was a rebirth, an instant shift; like my sexuality was handed back to me in an envelope.

important part of sex and I wondered if there were any solutions for FGM.

In 2017 I underwent restorative surgery. The package also came with therapy and a number of sessions with a sexologist.

It was a rebirth, an instant shift; like my sexuality was handed back to me in an envelope. The power that came with it also tore down the walls of religious beliefs and restrictions. I thought, *I am going to enjoy this.*

I would get back from work, sit with a mirror and look at myself. I thought, *I want to see this beauty.*

At the moment, I am seven months into a relationship with someone, and every time we have sex I enjoy it.

Oral sex has been the most humbling thing for me. I'd only had oral sex once before; I wouldn't accept it because it involved someone's face being down there. Now I am not scared of being seen. I just flip my feet like an open umbrella. *Take me. Take the whole of me, do your mighty.*

My partner knows how much pleasure I get from oral sex, and

I resist, the longer he has to work. *I want to stay here for the rest of my life!*

My orgasms feel like fireworks – they are explosive, one fit after another and another, like I am being electrocuted, until the biggest, and then I feel I'm going to die.

He alternates between oral and penetration, so I'm very aroused and wet. It's magic. I am in my own *Alice in Wonderland* world, seeing bubbles – no thoughts, just pure pleasure. It's a kind of blankness and in-the-moment-ness that I didn't know before.

This has been a time of fully assimilating what FGM had taken away from me and what potentially I would have missed out on for my entire life. But I have sadness about the women going through life with such struggles. I know that the story of my horrible sex life before is the story of many women.

Kim Thompson is a commercial illustrator and print artist based in Nottingham, England. Inspired by folklore, pop culture and a retro kitsch aesthetic, Kim's work centers on women and empowerment. ◉ @kim_a_tron

ILLUSTRATION BY KIM THOMPSON

I find sex fun. I laugh when I come; the bigger the orgasm, the more out of control my laughter.

— NOÉMIE

NOÉMIE

— 33 —

FRANCE

I find sex *fun*. I laugh when I come; the bigger the orgasm, the more out of control my laughter. This has often surprised my partners, usually in a positive way. I think it's because I feel like my orgasm is an explosion of joy in my body.

I'm still single, always in and out of relationships that usually last a few months or years. It's not the situation I long for. Most of the time, unfortunately, I use sex as a way to keep my partner interested, even if it's something I don't want to do anymore.

I have a high sex drive, which has been confused with 'easy'. In French there's a word – *coquine* – which means naughty, and I've been called this more than once. Sometimes I go more low-key with men, because I think when they see how much I like sex, they lose respect. I've felt like the more I gave sexually, the more detached the man became, this happened on the rare occasions I've experienced anal intercourse. I find it quite sad and unfair that women should have to repress their relation-ship to sex and especially the 'giving' part, in order to be respected. It's made me think that, well, we still live in a macho society despite appear-ances. Men still struggle with the Madonna/whore image.

As a child my family was very free, I was taught that sex and nudity were good and natural. I almost felt guilty about not talking about my own sexu-ality or my own body with my family.

I lost my virginity at sixteen and enjoyed it from the beginning. I always had sex with boys I loved. In my early twenties I wanted to con-quer as many guys as I could! But I could never sleep with strangers or have one-night stands, I was too much of a romantic.

And yet, although I grew up with the idea that sex was healthy, some-thing in my early sex experiences made me believe that a woman had to please a man through sex to be loved. I'm not quite sure why. Prob-ably because I had a very liberal but very overbearing and overshadow-ing father. Today, I'm just starting to really get out of the 'I'll be the best sex you've had so you'll love me more' pattern, and focusing on enjoying it, asking for what I love, and respecting my boundaries and limits.

I have a lot of images rushing through my head during sex. I usually

trust and am able to let go, then I can come when penetrated – but usually it takes more 'work'.

Afterwards I feel relaxed, happy and want hugs and kisses. Sometimes I feel sad if I know the relationship isn't going anywhere. I get attached

I think I'm an insecure woman in a man's world, who enjoys sex a lot and is trying to feel more empowered.

only come when having cunnilingus because it allows me to go to fantasy world. I'll often have a lesbian fantasy or I'll remember great scenes from my best sex with exes (not often, but it has happened) or I'll imagine a sex situation with a stranger. Sometimes, if the sex is really great, I don't need anything, and can just get lost in the moment.

I like soft, tender sex but also passionate sex. Speed turns me off though, even with oral sex – if it's too violent or speedy, I just switch off. Sometimes I also enjoy my hair being pulled and a little light spanking. I've been told I'm more 'fiery' than the image of myself that I project, which is angelic, sweet and soft.

I like penetration but it's not the most important part of sex for me as it's not the best way for me to climax. I don't enjoy quick or rough penetration. I'm quite sensitive and will bleed easily depending on the roughness of the act or size of the penis. For me, I think it's more about feeling trust with the partner. When I can

to someone as soon as the sex is really good and I worry that he isn't feeling the same.

I think I'm an insecure woman in a man's world, who enjoys sex a lot and is trying to feel more empowered.

Regards Coupables is an illustrator, graphic designer, musician and videographer based in Paris. Through his simple, clean-line illustrations, he likes to express a sense of tongue-in-cheek sexuality that gets right to the point.
@regards_coupables

ILLUSTRATION BY REGARDS COUPABLES

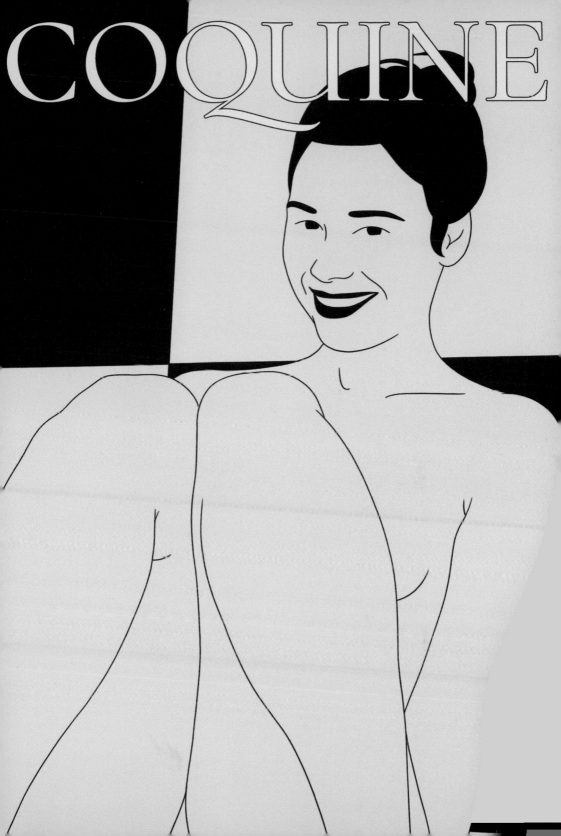

COQUINE

I don't think sexuality and disability is talked about enough.

— HOPE

HOPE

I don't think sexuality and disability is talked about enough.

My parents left me to figure it out on my own, but I really wish they'd said, 'Don't just date the first person who will have you,' because that's what I did.

I was called ugly all the time when I was little; I thought I might as well take what I can get. If I am disabled and ugly, then I might as well date people who want to date me. I got mixed up with people who weren't very nice to me and I always felt guilty for having a sexual relationship outside of marriage.

When I was fifteen I kissed a guy who was really popular, but I wasn't. We both knew that if other people found out it would be damaging to his reputation. I confided in one person I thought I could trust and she told everyone. The whole school knew about it but he denied it. Everybody thought I'd made it up; I got hate emails from people I didn't even know. His reputation was more import-ant than my feelings and the truth.

It took me a while to feel better about this but, for the most part, I do now.

I masturbate to help me sleep. I use a Hitachi vibrator, which is really good. It's always plugged into the wall. It's marketed as a back massager. I bought it initially because I had some severe back pain – and it is actually a really nice vibrating massaging tool to use on your neck or your shoulder – but I also knew that it was a sex toy, so I started using it for that as well. I mostly use it over my underwear as it can be a bit intense on my skin.

I fantasize about my ex-boyfriend, who I haven't seen for eight years. When we were together he didn't really have time for me – literally. The last time I saw him he had a time limit and was constantly look-ing at his phone and watch. I wish we could have had an experience where he wasn't thinking about the other things he had to do, or rushing off to his next appointment. In my fantasy, he makes time for me – not just for my benefit, but because it's something he really wants – and he penetrates me and it doesn't hurt.

Sex has always hurt for me. I have severe endometriosis and a retroverted uterus, which means my uterus sits over my rectum, not my vagina, but all this was only diagnosed last year. I don't think I have ever had fourth one, and the worst. He was very rough with me and he didn't slow down when I said, 'Please, be gentle, please, slow down, that hurts.'

I found the way he spoke to me even more hurtful than the physical assault. Everything was a command.

I've only had one partner who was very gentle and caring, and who listened to me when I said, 'That's enough,' but sex still hurt.

a pain-free sexual experience.

I've only had one partner who was very gentle and caring, and who listened to me when I said, 'That's enough,' but sex still hurt. It was then I realized that there might be something medical going on. One in ten women have endometriosis and one in five have a retroverted uterus but, kind and helpful as my gynecologist has been, he just said, 'Find a sexual position that doesn't hurt,' and I haven't found that yet.

I don't date. A few years ago my mum asked me why that was. I said, 'Because I get turned down for being ugly,' and she said, 'Date an ugly guy.'

I have noticed that, over the years, I will have a one-off with someone when I'm going through a period of grief. It happened a couple of months ago. I just didn't want to think about what was going on; I wanted to think about something else. I met him online. I had no interest in getting to know him, I said in the message it was just sex.

But it turned into an assault, my

Do this. Do this. I hadn't consented to be spoken to in such a demeaning way. He said things like 'Spit on my dick', which I would never do anyway.

A lot of people think that either people with disabilities can't have sex or just aren't sexual people. I saw a TED Talk by Danielle Sheypuk – she's a therapist who uses a chair – and she said, 'We have fabulous social circles, great careers, and loving families. But when it comes to our self-esteem, our dateable self-esteem, it's in the gutter.'

I am still struggling with this aspect of myself a lot.

Rachel Gadsden is a British artist who is exhibited internationally and who works across the mainstream and disability art sectors. Gadsden's work explores notions of fragility, survival and hope. She has a chronic hereditary lung condition and visual impairment; she is fitted with a syringe driver that injects her every minute with drugs to support her breathing. ◉ @rachelgadsden

ILLUSTRATION BY RACHEL GADSDEN

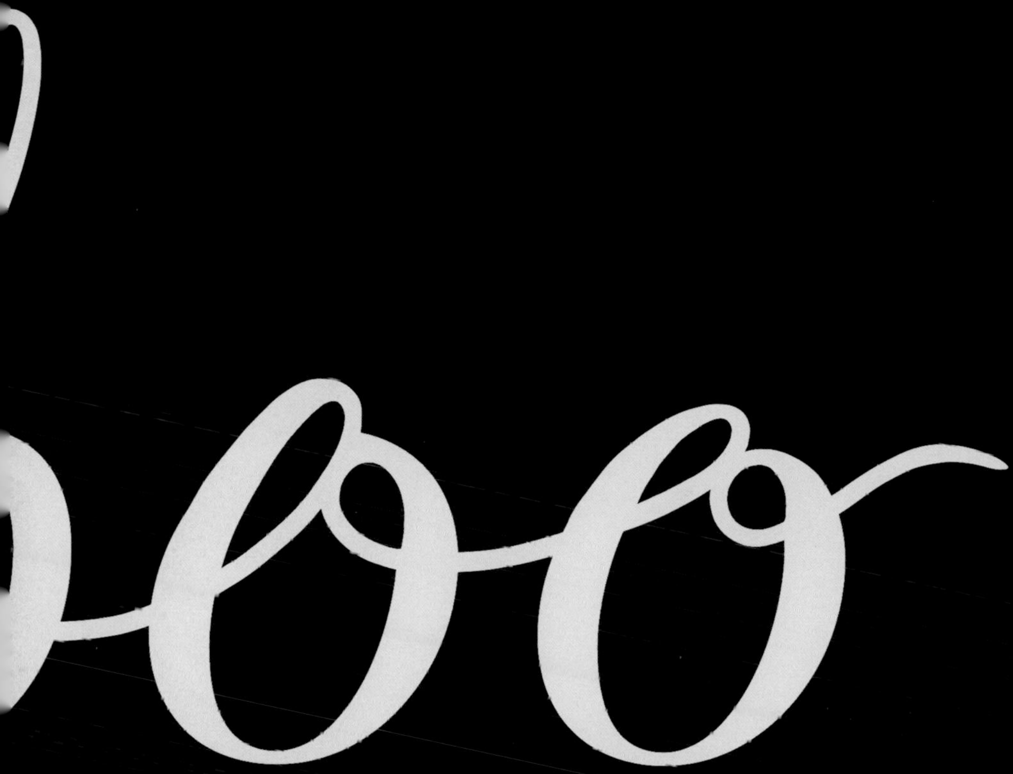

I'm single poly(amorous). I sleep with different people and have love and support from a girlfriend and a boyfriend. It is fucking magical.

— LINDA

LINDA

My favorite thing is to go to hotels. Hotels are for fucking.

If I don't have enough time, if I know there's only a two-hour window, or if someone is in the house, I'm just like, 'It's not worth it to go there and be halfway fiddling.' I really felt that with this dude recently.

I'm single poly(amorous). I sleep with different people and have love and support from a girlfriend and a boyfriend. It is fucking magical.

I like to be really free and very playful while I'm having sex: I like to play music and take a lot of pictures. I am very visual. I like to wear robes and try out toys, just kind of messing around. But I have to think about very practical things, like, *Can I be comfortable during sex? Do I have enough towels so I can soak the bed?*

I discovered I could squirt when I was thirteen by accident. I used to watch my parents' VHS 70s porn; they'd go shopping and I would put it on. Men with mustaches and white socks doing double penetration, which was fascinating to me. *Wow,*

how is this even possible? One day, I got a kitchen ladle with a nice round handle and thought, *This will work.* I squatted down with it while watching the porn and I squirted. I learned from an early age always to have a towel around.

At twenty-two, I trained as a tantric masseur. You learn that every cock is different and change is what works the best. It's good to vary what you do; unexpected, different touch, different speed, different intensity. It's not what works for me as a woman. I'm like, *Do one thing for half an hour.*

I love giving pleasure to a guy with my mouth. Most men really like to receive blow jobs; they can do nothing except surrender. I feel that there is a magical place that we access when we surrender and I want people to experience that. It's worship. I think, *Wow, I am really honored that you would let me do that.*

It's hard for me to surrender with cunnilingus. When it occurs, the first thing I think about is something that happened when I was eleven. My sister had a boyfriend who was very nice, and sometimes I would sit on his lap and we would cuddle. If my parents weren't home, he would undress me and lick me. I thought we were in a relationship and I was taking steps to becoming an adult. I knew I had to keep it secret because he was my sister's boyfriend. For a long, long time I

Last Saturday, my male lover said, 'How about I put on your strap-on and use my cock as well.' Prosecco happened, we tried it and it worked! He had to put the harness high up so it wouldn't squash his cock and balls. The dildo went into my pussy while he fucked my arse. I was like, *It works, it's possible!* It was very exciting.

> *With penetration I definitely feel the power of womanhood . . . How much our pussies are capable of: being fucked, having a baby, bleeding. When I think about it, I am so proud to be a woman and to experience such intensity.*

didn't know it was sexual abuse. Later I realized how my depression, my job, how sexual I have been since I was very young, is all connected.

The way my girlfriend licks me is so different to the way a man does it. It's spacious and gentle, and there is no agenda. I enjoy that; I came with the clit for the first time with her.

Because the VHS porn was something I saw a lot of, double penetration was definitely one of my fantasies. It's hard to find two men comfortable doing that though. It first happened about a year ago but it just didn't work – one of the men had trouble with his erection and his cock kept being pushed out. We were trying all sorts of positions. I couldn't walk the next day.

With penetration I definitely feel the power of womanhood. How we can take so much and be okay. How much our pussies are capable of: being fucked, having a baby, bleeding. When I think about it, I am so proud to be a woman and to experience such intensity and a huge range of emotions.

Sofie Birkin is a queer British artist currently living in Denver. She creates bold and diverse characters in lively, contemporary illustrations that aim to empower. She is the illustrator of two previously published books, *Sex Ed* and *The Art of Drag*.
@sofiebirkinillustration

ILLUSTRATION BY SOFIE BIRKIN

*I don't think I've enjoyed
sex for a long time . . .
I guess it's down to a
lot of factors, but mainly
I find it hard to shelve
'Mum' and be 'Lover'.*

— HOLLY

HOLLY

— 35 —
ENGLAND

I don't think I've enjoyed sex for a long time. When my husband and I were first together, I had a really high sex drive. We'd do role play, dress up, use toys, things like that. Sex was a big thing between us. But that has gone by the wayside. I guess it's down to a lot of factors, but mainly I find it hard to shelve 'Mum' and be 'Lover'.

By the end of the day, I have given myself to so many other people I'm knackered and just thinking about sleep. I'll usually be facing away from him towards the baby's cot. I still wear my nighties from when I was a size thirty; very big, they cover everything tent like. Great for breastfeeding, but it doesn't make me feel attractive.

He will put his arm on me or start stroking my leg. I tense up, wondering what excuse I can come up with. We probably have sex every week. Right now, it's been over a week because I had my period last week. Time is ticking. Often, after sex, I think, *That's a reprieve for a few days*, which is an awful thought.

He might do something in a jokey way to initiate things but I find that a big turn-off. He looked at me the other day and said, 'Go on, get your knickers off.' He says he's doing that because it hurts when I say no.

There's quite minimal kissing. He's got a beard now and it doesn't really do it for me. I should be honest and tell him.

I used to give him oral sex, not so much now. I have hang-ups. At school, I was always friend-zoned by the boys. That was a hard place to be and it plays on my mind still. At sixth form, there was one guy, I was in love with him, but he didn't feel the same. At a party, we fooled around in the bathroom, and I gave him oral sex. At the next party, one of his friends said, 'Do you want to go into this room?' and we did, and the same thing happened. At another party, a girl said, 'You know they're all talking about you and what they can get out of you.' It was spiteful but also an epiphany. In my head, with my husband, I feel like the seventeen-year-old sixth former. Strange that it's coming up now.

He'll go straight to going down on me. I might help myself to climax with my fingers. If I do, then I pull him towards me and want him inside me.

He often tells me to go on top, or he'll hug me and roll me on top. I really don't like how I feel in that pos-

the day after we have sex; he is much more demonstrative and loving, he'll tell me how he loves me. 'Isn't your mummy beautiful,' he'll say to the kids. He feels I'm not the ice queen. I am very stand-offish with him; it's self-preservation on my part in case

Penetration has made me emotional to the point of crying . . . It's an overwhelming amount of emotion to feel at one time.

ition. I can see myself and I have a lot in the way of loose skin and sagginess. I don't like my body on an aesthetic level and don't see why people would find it attractive. It has been changing constantly: I had a baby, was really ill with postnatal depression, and then two years later I had a gastric bypass. I lost eleven stone and then got pregnant again. I am astounded by what my body can do; it's grown and fed two amazing children. Often, I'll close my eyes so I don't see it, but then I won't look at him at all, which is such a shame.

Penetration has made me emotional to the point of crying. He will penetrate me and I will have tears in my eyes, but I turn away so he doesn't notice them; if he does, I play it down. It's an overwhelming amount of emotion to feel at one time. I realize I really do love him; I feel guilt that he's not my top priority now the kids are here, and for not doing enough for him. That's also mixed in with resentment that I have too.

His attitude to me is very different

he thinks he's in with a chance.

I would really just like some nice cuddles. He won't come and cuddle me just for the sake of it, only if it leads on to sex.

Jasmine Chin is an award-winning illustrator based in London. She creates playful and quirky illustrations inspired by popular culture.

@this_is_jasmine_chin

ILLUSTRATION BY JASMINE CHIN

I have dreams about me masturbating. In some I come, but in others I can't come; I masturbate and masturbate but I can't climax and it's very frustrating. I'm usually hiding, my mum is around the place and I'm really wanting to come.

— MONICA

MONICA

– 36 –

SPAIN

I've only come once with a guy. Usually I fake it, breathe a bit faster, make a bit of noise and say, 'Yeah, I'm done.'

The last time I had sex was a year ago, with my ex, Five-Minute Guy. In five minutes he'd come, then lay down and pick up his phone. He didn't put any effort into me at all. Each time this happened, I felt stupid. *What the fuck am I doing?* Afterwards he'd say, 'You want to come or not? You good?' *What kind of question is that? This is not the way you fucking ask!*

In my family, sex was never talked about. Questions weren't allowed; it's like you were supposed to be born knowing everything. I had to hide my boyfriends. But now I'm excited to be opening up and liberating myself. I have a friend, Orgy Guy – he's so free, he said, 'I have always been very sexual, I like to play and make people feel good.' It's inspired me.

I'm very horny. You wanna see my dildo?! It's a pink rampant rabbit. I like this little bunny a lot. Some weeks I don't want to leave my room.

I use my imagination thinking about the guys I am texting. I'm on Tinder. It's terrible; when I first opened it I was laughing the whole day. It's a meat market. It can go from saying hi to sending nudes very fast.

I had a sex dream about a guy I was messaging and I told him about it. He sent two pictures of his chest and a little bit of penis. His body language was super sexy. It made me hot and horny. Then he sent me a dick pic. I was like, *Fuck it, I'm going to send some photos, I want to do it, everyone is doing it, I don't want to be weird about it.*

I wore my sexy nightdress; it turned me on to keep some clothes on. I took the photo after I had masturbated, so my come was actually on my fingers. I played with mirrors for another one so you didn't see my face, just my whole back and butt. And there was one of me lying down in a sexy pose with my dildo next to me. It felt great to do this. I don't know why I'd had these barriers around doing it before.

One guy explained he was a cuckold; he wants to watch me have sex with someone else. He didn't seem like a weird pervert. He sent me some erotic stories and porn clips to show me what turned him on. I thought it was very interesting and exciting. I

I use fantasy more though, I can imagine way better than cheap porn.

It's intense with the dildo. I use it on my clit over my underwear, as it can be quite hard on my skin, especially when I change the batteries.

One guy explained he was a cuckold; he wants to watch me have sex with someone else. I thought it was very interesting and exciting. I really want to try it.

really want to try it. I think it will help me to open up.

I had a dream about this cuckold guy too. I was in a sexy dress, sat on a chair, going up and down on my dildo while he watched. I told him about it, and then he came here and we did that. I also put my dildo between his legs and sucked it. He said, 'This is hot,' and I said, 'Yes, for me too.' I came with my dildo.

Sometimes I watch porn. I go into Pornhub and stuff like that; it makes me horny but I think it's bullshit. It's all about what men think sex is. It feels like I'm having an experience with Five-Minute Guy.

I like Japanese porn. The guys aren't even having sex with the girl; they spend a lot of time with her using toys, and they get their pleasure just from giving her pleasure. Or I look for clips of forced sex in public places, although it's not really forced, obviously.

My orgasm feels like I am going to explode. I feel it and then I feel it again and then I feel it again. I come, come, come. I can be having an orgasm for a whole minute.

I have dreams about me masturbating. In some I come, but in others I can't come; I masturbate and masturbate but I can't climax and it's very frustrating. I'm usually hiding, my mum is around the place and I'm really wanting to come.

Bárbara Malagoli is a half Italian, half Brazilian illustrator based in London. Her work is all about compositions, shapes, vibrant textures and bold colors. ◉ @bmalagoli

ILLUSTRATION BY BÁRBARA MALAGOLI

I don't think that there is a person who isn't fond of receiving oral sex. Yes, yes, yes, please!

— SOPHIE

SOPHIE

– 36 –

IRAN

When I was a teen, sex was a taboo. We didn't have sex education and there was no internet; the older girls would tell stories to scare the younger ones, such as if you touch yourself, it leaves a mark on your private parts and no one will marry you.

In the shower, I would point the pressure of lukewarm water on my vagina and it would make me come.

Before marriage I used to date different guys and have one-night stands. I would have sex just to enjoy it, and was very active in learning new positions and styles to find out what I liked. I even made sexy costumes for myself – ribbons sewed together or sleeves stitched to a bra – as they weren't that easy to find in my country.

It was all spontaneous sex. Usually, I let the guy take the lead. I considered it a cultural thing, but if he didn't initiate it, I'd send him indirect signals, such as deeply gazing into his eyes or staring at his lips for a few seconds when he was talking to me. Then he would start touching me, gentle strokes on my hand, arm or

cheeks. Most guys would ask permission for their next move, kissing, and then fast-forward to undressing.

My sexual life drastically changed after my marriage.

I had to have make-up sex, sex to get pregnant, scheduled sex. It isn't pleasurable all the time, but that's life. The rough time in marriage came when I stopped feeling desire for my husband, and the sexless period when neither of us knew how to initiate it because we hadn't done it for so long. Now we have scheduled sex during our bad times, and sure, it's not the most enjoyable, but it avoids our sex life going downhill in our monogamous relationship.

When the time comes, we get ready, take a quick shower, brush our teeth and prepare my vibrator, the lubricant and some tissues. I change into some cute, sexy outfit and then we lie next to each other on the bed and start kissing right away.

I am extremely sensitive to touch. I love it when his body brushes against mine. My back and my thighs are the most sensitive. The gentler the touch, the more I enjoy it; the tricky part is making my partner understand how gentle I want him to be.

I don't think that there is a person who isn't fond of receiving oral sex. Yes, yes, yes, please! A soft and wet stroke of tongue is much more desirable on my intimate part than a guy with rough fingers thinking, *Faster is better.*

When I'm receiving oral sex, I think, *Oh my god, this guy is the most*

emotionless, then I've only done it as an exchange to receive it myself.

I've had an orgasm almost every single time that I've had sex, but I actively help myself to reach it. I have a vibrator that I let the guy use on me, if we can't do it any other way. It's not a big deal for me how it's achieved.

Normally, I enjoy the non-penetrative part of sex much better – soft touching and licking. During penetration I have all sorts of distracting thoughts that I never have during

When I wear a sexy outfit it's not to impress the guy, it's to get aroused myself. I often use mirrors to try to see myself in the angles that the guy sees me.

handsome and loveliest guy in the whole world. A ridiculous thought, as I've had it about every single guy who has ever gone down on me, but considering the sensitivity I have to touch I guess it's not that weird.

I often enjoy sex at a pace slower than most guys desire. I like studying them, all the nooks and crannies and curves of their body, and how it feels to touch. I want to have enough time to devour and save it all in my memory. Unfortunately, most guys aren't that patient.

I can't say that I've enjoyed every single time I gave oral sex. It depends on the guy, and his reaction. If he helps me do it better and shows his arousal, then I enjoy giving it to him, but with passive men who lie there,

other parts of sex. There have been many times when I wished the guy would come faster and let me go.

I really enjoy myself during sex. When I wear a sexy outfit it's not to impress the guy, it's to get aroused myself. I often use mirrors to try to see myself in the angles that the guy sees me. At one time, I thought, *Maybe I'm bisexual.* I tried it with a few women and I came to the conclusion that although I enjoy sex with women I am ninety per cent straight.

I believe sexual liberation is empowering.

Jemima Williams is a Welsh artist who lives in London. She works in paint, cloth and digital mediums. She is also a writer and a milliner.
◉ @jemimatheillustrator

Guys who do not know how to give pleasure need to be told. When I was with guys who didn't touch me right, I'd take their hand and show them, saying, 'This is how you touch me.'

— ZAYE

ZAYE

— 36 —

MALAYSIA

One of my guy friends once called me a nympho because I love sex so much.

'You need to get checked out because you're always having these desires,' he said.

'It's not wrong for women to be sexually active, and we're not supposed to be ashamed of it,' I replied.

Being a Malay Muslim I learned that there should be no sex before marriage because it would bring shame to my family. They believe that sex is precious and should only happen with the one person you love. But when I was growing up, I would tell my girlfriends that I wanted to find out what I liked, and if I didn't explore, how would I know?

My boyfriend and I have been together for eight years. People ask us why we aren't married or living together, and we say, 'Why should we when we have such a good companionship at the moment?' It's never been boring. We both have high libidos, I guess!

I love looking at him. He'll ask me why I'm staring. 'I'm just lucky,' I say.

'I love looking at every inch of you.' I really do love him.

I giggle when I want sex! Or I'll say it out of the blue.

'It's the middle of the day!' he'll say.

'What about it?' I'll reply.

We sext a lot: 'You're in your bed and I'm in my bed, so one of us is in the wrong bed,' or I'll take a photo of my lingerie and say, 'It's off, when are you coming over?'

If a man doesn't know how to kiss and caress a woman properly, slowly and gently like he adores her, it must be awful. Kissing and caressing are the keys. My boyfriend has such sweet kisses. I love it when he kisses and strokes me slowly down to my breasts. I enjoy each and every touch.

After he gets me horny and makes me wet, he might touch my clit or go down me. When he goes down on me I get all the orgasms! At times, he says, 'I'm not done yet,' and that will really turn me on but I push him away and say, 'It's my turn!' Then I kiss him down to his penis, enjoying his soft spots, his earlobes, nipples and tummy. When I caress his inner thighs, he moans, 'Oh dear,' then I go down on him until he can't stand it anymore. I love it. Sometimes I have to say, 'That's enough, I can't wait to have you in me!'

There have been times, and we do laugh about it, when I am so tied up at work that I start thinking about work

be turned on and have an orgasm, but only with him, not with previous guys.

We have discussed whether maybe I am so sexually active because I was exposed very young. I was sexually abused from the age of seven to twelve. My own brother touched me, he said he was teaching me. I only figured it out a couple of years ago; it came to me like a flashback and I

I told myself I can't change the past. I am what I am. I am very grateful that I had the greatest friends and sister around me to support me.

when I am going down on him. I tell him about it; I prefer to be honest, I tell him he needs to distract me.

Communication is the number one key to a good relationship. We talk about what he likes and what I like. Guys who do not know how to give pleasure need to be told. When I was with guys who didn't touch me right, I'd take their hand and show them, saying, 'This is how you touch me.'

When he looks into my eyes for that first thrust of penetration, I feel like I am the most special girl in the whole world. I like it when we take our time, without rushing or going anywhere.

He always ensures that I come as much as I want to before he comes, so I have a lot of orgasms, especially when I am on top, and when he plays with my breasts. It is very easy for me to

was shaking. I had to have therapy for a year. I had to talk it out. I told my brother I remember what he did; he asked for forgiveness. I guess we got through it.

I told myself I can't change the past. I am what I am. I am very grateful that I had the greatest friends and sister around me to support me.

The art of Alphachanneling is an holistic exaltation of sexuality. The anonymous artist, based in California, describes their work as 'carnal, explicit and provocative, but in the most gentle, graceful and reverential way'.
◉ @Alphachanneling

ILLUSTRATION BY ALPHACHANNELING

If I'm going to be self-pleasuring, I like to have a shower and perhaps smoke some weed to get myself in the mood.

— MARY

MARY

— 36 —

KENYA

My father told me and my sisters that we could do anything the boys could do. This was quite unusual for a Kenyan man, and I look back on it now with gratitude because it made me strong and confident.

My parents were strict churchgoers. No one told me about sex. I got the feelings very early. They were horny, sexual feelings and I didn't know what to do with them. In many ways it felt like I was searching and searching for years, trying to work out what they were about. I was adventurous, I wanted to explore these feelings, but the boys my age weren't yet interested. Older men were interested in me though.

Once, when I was very young, still in high school, I went to a man's house during lunchtime. I was looking forward to exploring these feelings with him, but when I got there it felt very wrong. He was insistent. Nothing happened, thankfully, and I left. I came away thinking that I should probably wait until I was a bit older to do this sort of thing. Four years later

I heard that this man had HIV. I was so relieved that I had got away that day, because I wouldn't have known about using a condom back then and I would have ended up ill too.

I'm not sure whether all African men have a high sex drive, but my Kenyan boyfriends wanted it every day or every other day and if I didn't want it too they would pester or force me into it.

My husband is European, and it's fifty-fifty whether I initiate sex or he does. We are very different in how we approach it though. He will take a lot of time preparing everything: he gets massage oil, lights candles and then he offers to massage me. Whereas I am more in the moment, I just go for it by touching him or kissing him a certain way.

If he says he's tired then I always understand; I remember how it felt when I was tired and was pestered for sex. If that happens, I take myself off with my sex toy. I had my first orgasm when I was thirty-one; it was with a sex toy and oh, it was the biggest feeling of satisfaction.

If I'm going to be self-pleasuring, I like to have a shower and perhaps smoke some weed to get myself in the mood. Then I watch porn. My tastes vary – at the moment I am enjoying

do. I could easily survive without it but we are two people and you have to consider the other person.

Edging really gets me going. My husband will play with my clitoris; he pushes me towards orgasm but then

It's been fun to introduce sex toys to my husband. When we get the toys out, we know no one is going to come out of this alive! It's do or die!

same-sex films, last week it was BDSM. I use my vibrator. I can orgasm easily lying on my back, although orgasms feel even more amazing when I am on all fours.

It's been fun to introduce sex toys to my husband. When we get the toys out, we know no one is going to come out of this alive! It's do or die! I was very attracted to him because he was so adventurous in bed and he has respect for me, he won't cross my boundaries. We have a great inner connection, the same love and sex language.

I like oral sex although I prefer receiving it. Although not if the guy expects you to perform. I had one partner who was all, 'I'm gonna make you squirt, I'm gonna make you come,' and then I just couldn't relax at all. It's only when I feel free and relaxed with a partner that I enjoy it.

I always insist we have oral sex first because I don't really like penetration that much. I do it because I feel that's what you are supposed to

he stops, and then he does it again and again; he keeps building and stopping.

A while ago I went and got a tantric massage with a happy ending; the way this person touched my body was crazy, crazy, crazy! The impact it had on me was so intense. The edging always takes me back to there, although in the fantasy it is always my husband doing it. I did have the masseur in the fantasy once but it turned me off.

When I am done I feel I could sleep for eight hours.

KaCeyKal! is an artist based in Detroit. He captures what he feels is the beauty of the human form through illustrations and paintings that create compositions that also seek to uplift black women. ◉ @kaceykal

ILLUSTRATION BY KaCeyKal!

WE'D DO R

DRESS UP,

THINGS L

— HOLLY

OLE PLAY,

USE TOYS,

KE THAT.

I must be broken.
I must be made wrong.

— MAI

MAI

I must be broken. I must be made wrong.

I have gynecological problems which have led to zero libido. It makes me feel so alone, like I am the only person in the world not having sex and feeling great, missing out on this thing that makes the world go round and sells everything.

I came quite late to sex, I was twenty-three or twenty-four. It hurt but I just thought that was how it was the first time. I had the worst UTI afterwards, I was peeing blood and throwing up in the street. No one had ever told me that you have to pee after sex. I called my mum; she said, 'Oh yeah, they used to call that the honeymoon disease, Nanny told me that.'

When I have sex there is a raw stinging and burning around my vaginal vestibule and also a deeper ache which might be connected to or could be from me tensing. For years I went to doctors in the UK and was told there was nothing wrong with me. 'It's all in your head,' 'You just need to be more confident, really,'

'Try drinking a bottle of wine before sex.'

Eventually, in America, I was diagnosed with vulvodynia. It might have been caused by the pill, or a lack of hormones that caused a certain area to atrophy, or it could be that some women are born with more nerve endings there. It could even be partly psychological.

I was offered treatments like a cream made from crushed chillies that blasts the nerve endings with so much pain they are numb for a while. Botox, which relaxes the muscles but can cause incontinence ('You might want to carry a spare pair of clothes with you'). Or full-on surgery, which was really expensive. My husband was like, 'These are your options? They are all awful!'

Last year I gave birth. We haven't really tried sex a lot since. Of course, I'm exhausted, but it's got to the point where it's almost a phobic thing. There have been times when my husband has come to kiss me and I have felt quite panicky and cornered.

Sometimes he can tell, and that must be awful, to go towards your wife and there be terror in her eyes. I am bracing myself for pain, but at the same time shame and disappointment.

My husband is wonderful but there are times that he feels angry with me and resentful. We've been living in this situation for some years now. I don't blame him. He has always different, but then it's this crushing disappointment. I'll be having sex and feeling utterly shit about myself, most of the time thinking, *I hope this ends soon, I hope he comes soon, I don't want this to last long.*

I want to figure out a way to raise my daughter to feel sex-positive, like sex is important but not so important she can't have fun with it and experi-

Every time there's always a little glimmer of hope that it will be different, but then it's this crushing disappointment.

been incredibly sexual; sex is like his interest in an intellectual way. Our third date was at the sex club Torture Garden.

At best once a week, but usually once every two or three weeks, we will touch each other and usually both orgasm. Most of the time, touch on my clitoris is okay and my breasts and nipples give me pleasure. But even if it has been lovely, afterwards I'll always be thinking, *But it's not proper sex, he probably wants proper sex, he probably thinks how bad it is that it's not proper sex.* I'm always looking at where I should be, or where I hope I could be, rather than focusing on the progress I've made.

If we have got to the point of having penis-in-vagina sex it's because we have been fooling around and I've wanted it, but the fantasy and the reality of it are nothing like each other. Every time there's always a little glimmer of hope that it will be ment. I want her to understand the gravity of it without it weighing her down because I think that is where I've gone wrong.

But I am going to keep trying and trying until things are at least a bit better. I am on my own little journey, reading books and trying to keep exploring this side of myself. I just hope I'm not stuck in the mud with my wheels spinning.

Naomi Vona is an Italian artist based in London. She combines photography, collages and illustration, and by using pens, paper, washi tape and stickers, she gives to every image a new life. ◉ @mariko_koda

   ILLUSTRATION BY NAOMI VONA

I have so much anger towards men who take advantage of women or use their 'dominant' preferences to be selfish and rough, and I wonder sometimes if that anger is towards myself and the type of man I would perhaps be.

— JESSICA

JESSICA

— 36 —

CANADA

I used to worry that if I had sex with a guy too soon he wouldn't respect me. Now I joke to friends that having sex on the first date is my strategy to weed out the type of men I don't ever want to see again. I've embraced the term ethical slut.

I grew up in rural Canada and my family was very religious. Sex was always a shameful topic and sex education avoided. I learned about sex when I was around seven; my ten-year old male cousin told me about it, then wanted to try it with me. I remember resisting and him continuing to pressure me, then I have no memory of what happened after. It's always bothered me that I don't remember.

Five years later I found out he was molesting and raping my younger sisters. I carried guilt with me for many years because I never told anyone that he tried it with me. By confessing this and sharing it with other women of the world, I'm officially, finally taking the label of a victim, not perpetrator, which I felt for so many years I was.

Putting that to one side, I think I have had a pretty open attitude towards sex ever since I tried masturbating with a showerhead when I was around ten and it blew my mind!

I love my hair and the back of my neck stroked, my feet touched, and my stomach is almost as sensual as my breasts. Lately I've started realizing that I also like sex to be a bit more rough – my ass slapped, hands around my throat, held down, that kind of thing.

A man simply identifying as being dominant used to make me angry, now I'm realizing I'm very attracted to dominant men. I'm really torn on this one though. Even if I enjoy submitting, there's an emotional currency that I pay, which gives too much of me to them. It's all fairly new to me, and my gut says to walk the other way and not go further down that path at this time. I'm intrigued by the subject though.

When I first start giving oral sex, it really turns me on. But after a while,

I'm like, *Okay, I hope he comes soon now. My leg is cramping, is this guy coming yet? Oh, for fuck's sake, come already.* I say seven minutes should be the legal limit.

When I was younger I couldn't enjoy cunnilingus; all I could think about was if I smelled down there, if I tasted okay, if he was too close to my asshole. Now I do, if it's done right. Often when I'm receiving, I'm just trying to come. I'll run fantasies through my head to help me come faster. I get impatient if they take too long, and I'm assuming they're thinking the same.

I definitely enjoy penetration, although it depends on the position. If my clit isn't stimulated, it's not even that pleasurable, and I'm wishing he would come so I can have a cup of tea. If I'm in a position where my clit is engaged, I might close my eyes and have sexier fantasies than the current sex I'm having. If the sex is really good, I stay in the moment and don't fantasize about anything else.

One thing that bothers me sometimes is that some of my fantasies are a bit troubling. Sometimes I'm the man, with a penis, and I'm having sex with a girl. I'm not gay or bi even; the fantasy of having a penis just makes me come faster. It can be beautiful – I pleasure her and then have sex with her.

Other times the fantasy goes quite dark; she's quite vulnerable and I'm rough with her. I've had a fantasy where I'm on top of a very high water tower with a cute girl. I'm having sex with her from behind and she's terrified, leaning over the railings really high off the ground. I tried to climb this water tower once in real life and it scared me, I had to come back down. I have no idea why that ended up in my library of fantasies. I have so much anger towards men who take advantage of women or use their 'dominant' preferences to be selfish and rough, and I wonder sometimes if that anger is towards myself and the type of man I would perhaps be.

One thing that bothers me sometimes is that some of my fantasies are a bit troubling.

Emily Marcus is an illustrator based in Massachusetts. She is interested in telling stories that explore nature, and constructing fantastical places that exist beyond reality. She works primarily in gouache, clay, and the digital form. ◉ @emilplee

ILLUSTRATION BY EMILY MARCUS

Sometimes I focus on the light in the room and then close my eyes and carry it inside my body, and journey it to my vagina.

— CELESTE

CELESTE

– 38 –

COLOMBIA

I am a very intense person with a lot of energy and passion.

I'm married but from the beginning I had the feeling that ours was a natural open relationship.

After the birth of our child I was so scared of getting pregnant again I didn't want to be touched or have sex. I was like a nun for two years. I experienced such depersonalization at becoming a mother, I didn't think I had the strength to go through it again. I said to him, 'Don't close yourself to opportunities of getting involved with someone.' I knew I wasn't the only one who could make him happy - on the contrary, sometimes I've made him miserable.

Also, my body wasn't the same; some muscles in my vagina were damaged because my daughter had been too big to deliver naturally. For some time now, I've been doing pelvic exercises to help repair it and I've decided that I'll also have surgery to make the hole a bit smaller.

I have two ways of living my sex life now; it's like my life is made up of two sides. In one side, I go to BDSM play parties in Berlin where I have mostly play lovers. In these kinds of relationships, I fulfill fantasies and explore different roles. I used to have a pattern where I was always submissive and receiving, then at my first Xplore I went to a playground for adults and discovered that I was a natural dominatrix; part of my character says what she wants and how she wants it.

In Colombia, there are no play parties and finding lovers is very different. So here is where I live out my other side: I do it through dancing. It's very Catholic here in Latin America, but we also have a strong influence of passionate-love-only-hurts drama with the telenovela, the boleros and salsa.

You let go and give yourself to the other in the salsa. It's choreographed; you have to follow rules and steps, and it's very patriarchal; the man always leads. But sometimes you can change this pattern and propose a twist so he understands that you can lead too. If I dance fluidly with somebody and we become one in the dance I intuit that we could also be good in bed. The smell of a salsa partner can also really turn me on and make me hot. I try to grab him so

that only brings frustration.

When I am having sex I think of my body filling with light. Sometimes I focus on the light in the room and then close my eyes and carry it inside my body, and journey it to my vagina.

If I dance fluidly with somebody and we become one in the dance I intuit that we could also be good in bed.

he knows I want him and that I'm not shy or hiding anything.

There was one beautiful guy I met through the dance; I got the feeling he was nervous to be with me. He was huge. I saw him naked in this hotel room and I said, 'Wow, you are so fragile,' and he said, 'I am a two-metre-tall black guy, no one in my life has ever said this to me, but I am afraid to disappoint you.' I think it turned him on that I was so honest with him.

The truth heals everything. That is now my prayer and how I want to manage all my relationships. You can build so many masks and lies in your life.

One of my key moments in my sexual journey was with a woman. To be touched and appreciated by another woman is wonderful. I didn't know that my vagina could feel so much. Sometimes I think of her when I am having sex; she brought so many beautiful memories to my body. I didn't climax with men before her. We broke up because I wasn't lesbian. I was still looking for men. I couldn't give to her what she expected and

If there are birth marks or dots on the other person's body, I study and remember them and I imagine that they remember me, then when I close my eyes I see them as a constellation of stars.

Or I try to make an imaginary ball of light and move it all over my body. I once did this in a collective guided masturbation with 200 people. It was really a meditation. We all came at the same time. It was one of the most beautiful moments of my life. I felt loved and accepted, so free.

I think, if you are conscious about it, sex can be a meditation and each relationship with a lover can offer you a certain medicine.

Sabrina Gevaerd is a Brazilian illustrator based in London. She likes to explore the intersection between life and magic, with elements that range from female features to animals.
@sabrinagevaerd

ILLUSTRATION BY SABRINA GEVAERD

We have been married for God knows how many years. When we have the urge, it doesn't take very long, we've got cleaning to do!

— LING LING

LING LING

– 38 –

CHINA

Before I had a child, I was on top of the world, fully employed and successful, in control and confident. Now, I'm trying to be a mum and make a new life but I haven't worked out who I am yet. I've lost quite a lot of confidence and it's impacted my sex life in quite a negative way. It's as though I'm in this shell and I don't want to be discovered.

We have been married for God knows how many years. When we have the urge, it doesn't take very long, we've got cleaning to do! It's very ad hoc: the other day we had sex twice in a day, but then it can be several weeks between times.

Often, I need it during the day when I am more energetic physically. I get an itchy, horny feeling, and want penetration and the release of an orgasm. I don't know what triggers it, but I know I have to be in a happy mood. I used to think I'd save it for another time, but then another time comes and you aren't in the mood, so now as soon as I have the feeling I go for it.

I initiate by saying, 'I want to have sex right now.' I'm very direct; I've been living in the UK for twenty years and I still don't get all this going around the houses. I operate on a schedule, literally in five-minute chunks, next thing done, tick. I'm direct with what I want and I need.

I don't like snogging. You see it in the movies, but I don't understand why they do it. Sometimes I do it because I think it's what you're supposed to do. I've said this to my husband; he hates me saying it and I feel like a terrible person, but kissing is like a tumble dryer going around and around.

If we're on the sofa, he'll have his trousers halfway down his legs and I'll be fully naked straddling him. I like my boobs touched and to be held really close. We used to have foreplay, but I don't think we've done anything like that since I gave birth.

Quite often scenarios pop into my head and I imagine I'm being sexualized, perhaps being backed into a corner or raped. I could be a sex worker, or a schoolgirl who has been taken advantage of by a teacher, or a Japanese businessman. I've never questioned why I have these fantasies or thought whether it's right or wrong; they help me to enjoy the sex.

There's no oral sex anymore. I never liked my husband doing it to me anyway – I thought too much about it and my thoughts overcame

When I was young and having lots of orgasms, I always considered myself lucky. I'm guessing that my mum probably doesn't get orgasms. I would think that there are a lot of women like my mother, where perhaps sex is just purely a thing for the guy.

I've never heard Chinese people talk about sex – like, never. I went to

When I was really young I let him come in my mouth. It happened a few times, but I hate it, hate it, hate it.

my pleasure. I used to do it on my husband. I probably would still do it if he wanted it or if I was in the mood.

When I was really young I let him come in my mouth. It happened a few times, but I hate it, hate it, hate it. I think it's so wrong. There is no equality. I'll probably never do it again. If I did, I would be belittling myself. I'd feel I was in Thailand giving someone a massage with a happy ending, and for me that isn't a good thought. I don't judge women who do it, but for me, if I had to do something like that, I would have had to have reached rock bottom in my life. I'd think we weren't equal, and I need to have an equal relationship in my sex life.

I orgasm within a few seconds and I can have several of them at once. My orgasm comes from inside, it's mind-blowing. I see sunshine. For a moment I can't think about anything – not bad thoughts, or good thoughts, nothing but pure pleasure.

one of the best high schools in my city and everyone was focused on studying and getting to the top of the class; there were zero conversations about boys getting together with girls. I didn't have any sexual education and there was nowhere to find out about it. I wasn't going to ask my parents.

For my generation, my mum's generation and those above, it's a thing we don't talk about. But that's changing – recently I've heard some podcasts where sex is discussed.

Jasmine Chin is an award-winning illustrator based in London. She creates playful and quirky illustrations inspired by popular culture.
@this_is_jasmine_chin

ILLUSTRATION BY JASMINE CHIN

I wouldn't want anyone to have less love than they could possibly want because they are in a relationship with me.

— JENNIFER

JENNIFER

– 39 –

USA/UK

I'm a few years into the medical side of my transition. My testosterone is suppressed with medication so it's lower than it is for the average cis-gender woman but I haven't had any surgery yet.

I really like the drop in testosterone. I don't have a hormonal impetus making me horny now; rather, it comes from feeling safe with someone – lots of cuddling, kissing and laughter – and I enjoy that. I have much less sex, but when I do, it's a really special experience; it takes longer and is sensitive and emotional. I don't really miss the way I used to have sex.

I have one partner who I've been with for four years, and another coming up for two. I also have some long-term cuddle buddies; they're also partners but in a more platonic and affectionate way. It's a chosen family, everyone is interlinked with each other. I've been polyamorous for fifteen years; I wouldn't want anyone to have less love than they could possibly want because they are in a relationship with me.

And I love it when there are more than two people being intimate – all the shared energy and happiness is really beautiful. It means I can relax, stroke or kiss someone or give them head, but have a more chilled out or lackadaisical role sexually.

I really enjoy a slow progression of gentle stroking, a long dance towards going down on someone. Kissing the bottom of someone's stomach, the curve around a hip, the small of a back. I like to hold someone while that is happening, wanting them to feel held and loved. Hearing their voice is a big turn-on for me, someone telling you what they want you to do or what they're enjoying. I make lots of little happy whimpering noises.

I've always seen myself as a bit like my mother, someone who looks after people. I'm not good at wanting things for myself or feeling that I am entitled to things and that means, in sex, I've tended to share intimacy around me by giving, and been slightly uncomfortable when there is a disproportionate amount of attention on me.

I like gentle strokes on my bum, my sides, the inside of my thighs, stomach, neck, collarbone and boobs. I really like my boobs. I haven't had these for most of my life, and now I've finally got them I am just thrilled. I'm joining the itty-bitty-titty committee, as my partner would say.

When I receive oral sex now, the physical sensation is a lot different; it's sensitive but not always inherently pleasurable. I will need a nar-

properly, but also not really wanting it to. A lot of guys are really into giving blow jobs to trans women, but I just didn't want that, it didn't feel like the feminine energy I had was being seen. They were singling out that part of me which I still thought was the masculine bit, and I didn't like that.

Over time, though, I had experiences of being naked at parties, and saw and befriended women with penises and talked to them about their gender identity. They didn't see it as a masculine part – one friend

Talking about the penis is quite difficult for trans women . . . I generally have to take medication if I want to have any erection.

rative going on in my head, which is emotional and centers on feeling wanted, attractive and comfortable with someone, and I have to focus on that. If I am going to climax, it will be a long process with lots of that thought involved, but if I am anxious or stressed it won't be possible.

Talking about the penis is quite difficult for trans women, unless they are talking to each other. People think it's exactly the same organ as it is for a cis guy, but it's not. I generally have to take medication if I want to have any erection. Over time, a woman's penis will tend to get smaller and start to smell or taste more like a cis person's vagina than it used to.

I've always had a difficult time using my penis. I had a weird disconnect, feeling like it didn't work

called hers a 'girl dick', another a 'lady cock' and another said she had a big clit.

There is a lot of hatred of trans people at the moment. I am very aware of how people see me; I have a lot of fear and a lot of shame. I think I've reacted to people's disgusted and aggressive reactions to something they see as freakish.

But I have an amazing community around me. I think I must be one of the luckiest trans women in the country.

Chrissie Hynde is the singer and songwriter of the band The Pretenders. In her spare time, she paints colorful still life, portraits and expressive abstracts. www.chrissiehynde.com

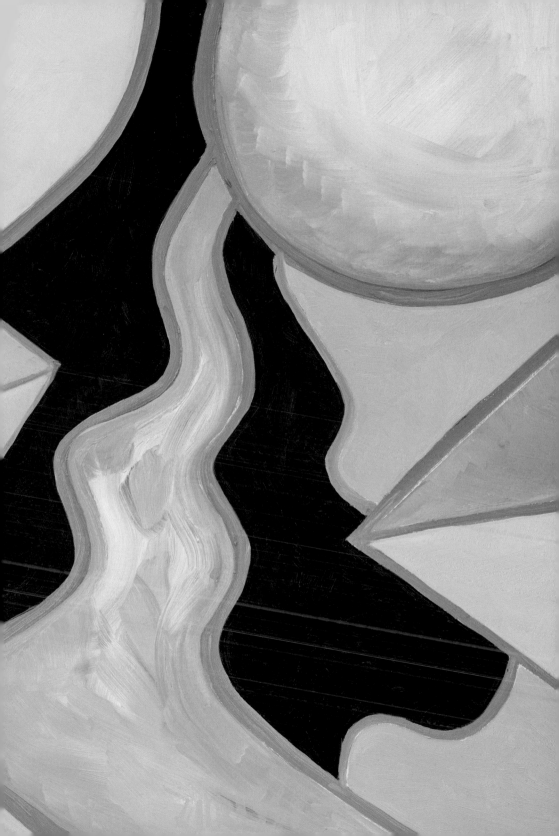

Marriage is very respected; everyone wants your marriage to succeed and not fail. When a couple have troubles in their marriage and it becomes public knowledge, people say, 'Didn't they get the teachings?!'

— PRISCILLA

PRISCILLA

— 40 —

TANZANIA

When I started my period, my grand-mothers were brought in to explain menstruation to me and some of my female cousins. We were also taught that we would have to genitally mod-ify ourselves in preparation for sex.

Different tribes do different things. With my dad and mum's tribes nothing is cut, but you're expected to pull the skin at the base of your vagina and rub it with a black powder of herbs. It elongates your lips and is supposed to bring sexual pleasure to the man. In the olden times and even now sometimes, at the marriage negotiations the husband's family can ask, 'Is she completely prepared for our son?' and some will even demand to check.

Me being the little diva, the little feminist, I was like, 'Hang on! Why is it all about the man?' In my culture, you're not supposed to question an elder, just listen and do what they say. My other cousins did what they were asked to do, but I refused. Some-one told my father. He knew about this practice, of course, because my mum had followed it, but he said, 'I think it's a whole bunch of hocus-po-cus, she's not doing it.'

My father raised me to be con-fident, fearless and to reach for the stars. He made the difference. He was open and honest: 'If you are going to engage in sex,' he said, 'make sure you are safe, ideally love the person, know their HIV status, and if they got tested.' In Southern Africa, rates can be as high as one in four people being HIV positive. I've lost a lot of family members to the disease.

Sex has to mean something for me to find it pleasurable. I think men and women are wired differently. For men, eventually it becomes emo-tional, but for the most part, it's phys-ical; for me, it has always been emo-tional.

My husband and I have busy lives revolving mostly around the children, so we're always tired. We joke about it: 'Not today, mate, I'm out of order.' Sex doesn't happen often, but when we do it's very heartfelt and passion-ate because our love is deeper.

I used to have a high sex drive, but it tapered off after my first child. I find that when I have kids, especially the first year, I don't feel very sexual at all. Particularly when I am breast-feeding. I feel torn between belonging to the baby and belonging to my husband.

When we have sex, it usually hap-

happy, all those emotions into one.

We had the traditional marriage teachings before our wedding. I was taught by women, my husband by men. Some of it was very useful: how to keep a home, how to manage arguments, what to do when children come along. I was taught about sex, and how to physically gyrate to

It's hard to explain my climax. It's like water builds up internally and is about to burst, but in a nice way.

pens in the morning between 4 a.m. and 8 a.m., before the kids wake. I like to touch his face and his ears; it's intimate for me there, I get to be close and can express how I feel about him. I try to be in the moment, seeing his reactions; if he perks up and recipro-cates then I know I am doing the right things.

Foreplay is very important; it helps my body prepare itself for penetration. Otherwise it hurts. Kissing my breasts and touching my clitoris simultaneously, that kills me, then I'm happy, but I don't like having an orgasm before intercourse. When I'm wet and ready, I'll either say so or gesture. I'll be heightened at this point and he will penetrate me slowly. We might verbalize our love: 'I love you' or 'I appreciate you'.

It's hard to explain my climax. It's like water builds up internally and is about to burst, but in a nice way. At the end we cuddle or have a long embrace. I feel tired, but also fulfillled, lucky,

please him – a lot of it is about shaking your waist and moving slowly down and up. I use those moves sometimes. They work.

Marriage is very respected; every-one wants your marriage to succeed and not fail. When a couple have trou-bles in their marriage and it becomes public knowledge, people say, 'Didn't they get the teachings?!'

I could never cheat on my hus-band. I hope he knows that. It would mess me up emotionally, and phys-ically I couldn't do it. So far, I have learnt that how you conduct your relationship with your partner is linked to your sexual relationship as well. If you can stay connected in all areas of your relationship, then your sexual one is bound to be healthy too.

Ojima Abalaka is an illustrator based in Abuja, Nigeria. Her works explore rest, people and identity in the context of everyday life. ◉ @ojima.abalaka

ILLUSTRATION BY OJIMA ABALAKA

Culturally in Zimbabwe, women are taken aside at a certain age and told to elongate their labia and put herbs inside their vaginas to make them firmer for the man, hence we have the highest rates of cervical cancer.

— RUDO

RUDO

— 41 —

ZIMBABWE

I'm in the middle of a break-up.

The domestic pressures of a relationship can ruin the love, and therefore the sex. The daily things become all you see about your partner, until you can't imagine having sex because they haven't washed the dishes. I had no concept that things could fall apart so much.

He was the best sex I ever had. In the beginning my orgasms made me feel as if I was floating above my body. It was extraordinary. In retrospect, I know now it wasn't so much technique as people coming together with chemistry.

But sex became really boring and repetitive. I enjoyed his touch when we weren't in a sexual mode, but if he was feeling amorous, he'd suddenly become very heavy-handed. It was like this performance. He would initiate by starting to touch me, but it wasn't soft or caressing. I would roll my eyes in the dark, feeling tired, thinking, *You woke me from my sleep and I have an early start.*

It took a while for me to put it into words and explain to him that I liked soft caresses, little kisses, a build-up. But then he would say, 'I'm trying, I'm trying to do it like you said and you're not responding.' I think he was trying but I didn't feel his heart was in it. It felt like it was something he needed to do before he put his penis in me. I wanted him to put time and initiative into it. Read about it, do some research. Google is free! But he didn't take the time. I'm still trying to process it.

He refused to give me oral sex, but he would expect it from me. At first, I wasn't thinking of it too much, then I was like, *Wait a minute!* I brought it up, and he said, 'Yes, yes,' but then he didn't do it. Oral sex is something that is very western; I think it's a phenomenon that has been introduced through porn. For women in Zimbabwe it's mostly not an option that is on the table. It's only really people who are middle class and above doing it; if you are lower class, it's considered gross. If you are lower class you have less exposure to Western ideas, and your understanding of sex tends to be through your elders and your aunties, rather than popular culture. When you are middle or upper middle class, like me, you don't live in a rural space or a township-identity space, your aunties aren't around to give you a sex talk; you get it through movies, your peers and triple-X videos.

Zimbabwean men aren't taught how to please women. We've spent hundreds and thousands of years being the ones who provide pleasure.

When I was younger I was abused by several people. It makes me angry that people don't understand how vulnerable children are. For a long time, I carried the weight of it. I'd walk down the street and be sexually harassed; I'd get wolf whistles and comments, and it would freak me out so much.

Then there was a colleague at work who crossed the line. I reported it and a week later I was fired. But I took them to court and won. Ever

In my experience, the larger the penis, the worse he is in bed because he thinks he's won the lottery and everyone will be happy.

Culturally in Zimbabwe, women are taken aside at a certain age and told to elongate their labia and put herbs inside their vaginas to make them firmer for the man, hence we have the highest rates of cervical cancer. I didn't have to do this, but I remember when we were young my cousin pulled me to her, saying, 'Ooh, I want to show you something.' I was like, 'What? This is ridiculous.'

Zimbabwean men are taught that if you have a large penis, you pound a woman to death and they are happy with it. But in my experience, the larger the penis, the worse he is in bed because he thinks he's won the lottery and everyone will be happy. But that is not how it works.

I would be pounded. It was sore, I wasn't lubricated and I'd be thinking, *Why does this keep happening?*

since then I've felt more in control of my sexuality and my body, like I could say no for that child in me who couldn't.

Now, I want something more, someone who isn't stuck in this binary male-versus-female, someone on a journey of discovery, of sexuality. I don't know whether I will ever find that person, but it's something I have begun to dream about, who knows.

Destiny Darcel is an artist based in Atlanta. She currently balances working as a software engineer, designer and illustrator, focusing on celebrating black women. 🄾 @destinydarcel

ILLUSTRATION BY DESTINY DARCEL

I remember at a young age, maybe seven, riding a bike and feeling aroused and thinking, 'I can do this to me!'

— BOUDICEA

BOUDICEA

— 42 —

UK

I made a promise to myself that I wasn't going to sleep with anyone unless I really loved them. I haven't had intercourse for five years.

I've always found relationships difficult. My mum brought three kids up on her own. Typical West Indian parent – whether she wanted to or not, she had to become a strong woman because her husband left her.

We were brought up Catholic and we used to go to church every Sunday. I was going to say that sex was a dirty word, but actually my mum was very comfortable telling us not to have sex. She gave us the sex talk when I was about six or seven, and there was no mucking about, no fluffy words – it was 'penis' in 'vagina' and 'you don't want to get pregnant because I have made so many sacrifices'. This message of *don't have sex, don't get pregnant* underpinned everything in my approach to relationships.

I think I have dated every single type of guy, but there are only two or three I had an emotional connection with. I treasure that, the effortless conversation and loving, caring and fun sex, and the fact that they saw me how I am. I've felt like a novelty act before: 'I've never dated a black girl.' 'Do all black guys have big willies?' It was as though I was being tested out.

I remember at a young age, maybe seven, riding a bike and feeling aroused and thinking, *I can do this to me!* I've been touching myself from the age of thirteen or even younger; it seems as though DIY has always been part of my life.

I probably do it more when I am due on. I'll do my normal night-time routine, get a bit of essential oil going, turn on my salt lamp and get into bed. I don't sleep naked; I don't like being cold and I have the most irrational fear that something is going to climb up my vadge. I've also got big boobs, so I wear a sleep sports bra. If I want a quick fix, I will get the vibrator out, but if I feel like taking my time, I'll switch on my fantasy and finger myself. When I am not using a vibrator, I find it easier to come on my front rather than on my back.

Sometimes I think I have too many fantasies, although I'm pretty sure you can't have too many.

One I go to a lot is where four men please me. We can be in a house, hotel, outside, wherever, I'm not fussed. I don't really see their faces; really hard.' Classic cliché stuff.

My vibrator is teeny tiny and a bit pathetic. I want to treat myself to a really nice one one day. I'd happily spend £150–200 because I know I'm going to get a lot of use out of it. I think of it as self-care and self-love – I

Sometimes I think I have too many fantasies, although I'm pretty sure you can't have too many.

it's more about the bodies, what they are doing and how they are using their hands and their willy wonkas. Physique-wise, the guys have to be defined but not bodybuilders. I'm quite healthy and I go to the gym, so it makes sense that the men in my fantasies look after themselves too. They have nice bums and other things! Interestingly they are more likely to be white than black.

I do have one fantasy where there are a lot more men, and in this scenario they are a mix of white and black. In that one, I am a high-powered exec being driven home in my limo. I have an all-male staff and their only instruction is that I come. When I arrive home, they are all lined up on the stairs and desperate to help and be the special one that will please me. I might pick one or they'll all come towards me.

Vaginal and anal penetration occurs. A normal routine would be playing around with the holes – in the vagina, then in the anus, then in both. I say, 'I'm a dirty bitch,' or 'Fuck me

realized in my mid-thirties that holistically you have got to love yourself.

My orgasm goes through my body with tingles and vibrations. I feel it everywhere, but sometimes it's very strong in my heart area. It is a lovely feeling, comforting and life-affirming.

Women's bodies are amazing. There are so many societal and religious issues surrounding sex, but it is our biggest power.

Kim Thompson is a commercial illustrator and print artist based in Nottingham, England. Inspired by folklore, pop culture and a retro kitsch aesthetic, Kim's work centers on women and empowerment. @kim_a_tron

ILLUSTRATION BY KIM THOMPSON

I've been with my husband for a long time. There's been beautiful growth in our sex life.

— KATE

KATE

— 43 —

NEW ZEALAND

I've been with my husband for a long time. There's been beautiful growth in our sex life.

When our children were young, our sex life was pretty sad. He'd initiate as I was about to go to sleep by pressing his hard cock against me. 'I'm not into it,' I'd say. He'd roll over but there would be no cup of tea the next morning. If we didn't have sex for too long, he'd get grumpy and sulk. As a mother, your body is touched all the time; you get to the end of the day and think, *I'm exhausted, the last thing I want is another body to take care of.*

I was conscious that his sex drive was stronger than mine, but only when I was having pedestrian sex. If I was enjoying it, then I was more likely to want it and initiate it. We started making more of an effort, having date nights and turning off Netflix.

My husband is turned on by me dressing up in the beautiful, ridiculously skimpy, sexy underwear he buys me. It's kind of fun for me but it won't turn me on. I thought, *What do I need?* And the answer was *heaps of talking.* I want to know what's going on in his mind. So I created this game where we put questions in a bowl; we have to answer a question, then we roll a dice which gives you tasks to do, like taking off an article of clothing or dancing. I was getting that deep intimacy I craved, and he was getting me to gyrate around the room for a while.

Getting away from that roll-over-in-bed initiation has been massive. Now he might put some super cheesy James Brown on and do a crazy sexy striptease. He'll have a pair of pants over a stripper G-string; it makes me laugh and laugh.

Or sometimes at 10 p.m. he'll say, 'I'm going to have a wank' and that's always okay for me. I love lying next to him and feeling his body, all tense. It's so powerful, it jolts through my body. Sometimes he'll watch porn or we might tell each other fantasies.

I like getting into a fantasy state. They tend to take place somewhere hot – an island with a beach and palm trees. Beautiful naked bodies, often two guys – sometimes one of them will be my husband, not always, although I always tell him it is! I will be the center of attention, sexual, powerful and admired.

I love touching his body, his chest, his arse, the soft tissue under

touch us. I never wanted to say hello to grandad. When I was eleven, I put dungarees on and a sweatshirt over them because I knew he would put his hand up my top but I knew it wasn't okay to say no. He humphed when he couldn't feel anything, and I felt very

I may get out my vibrator and we'll lie wanking beside each other.

his balls, hearing him respond to my touch, feeling him get hot and sweaty. Sometimes I love taking his cock in my mouth when it's soft and feeling it go hard.

For me I like lots of touch on my neck and little tender kisses all down my body. But I dissociate myself quite a lot and find myself thinking about irrelevant stuff, like my kids' lunch-boxes. I try and stay present by thinking, *Come back here.*

I may get out my vibrator and we'll lie wanking beside each other. Often we'll end up having sex.

I can't orgasm unless it's with a vibrator. I'd just decided it was my broken body, but now I'm wondering whether maybe I haven't properly been connecting with the feel of it. Recently I heard Peter Levine talk about sexual healing; he takes people through a free-touch exercise. When I do this it's like I am feeling my body properly for the first time ever. I think this being frozen out of my body might relate to some unwanted touch I had as a child.

When I was young my grandfather used to put his hands up our tops and

triumphant. It was the last time he tried to do that.

I grew up in such a conservative Catholic family, where even thinking about sex was bad. When I was four-teen I had a fantasy that I was raped. I thought about this recently; why would I imagine something so hor-rible? Then I worked out it must have been because if I was being raped and penetrated by a bottle, then it wasn't my choice; it didn't mean I was sinning.

Alice Skinner is a London-based illustrator and visual artist. She creates tongue-in-cheek and digestible images as a social commentary on 21st-century life. ⊙ @thisisaliceskinner

I fell in love and got married. We had lots of sex that in my opinion was really shit. It worked for him, it didn't work for me. I thought I was damaged.

— JASMINE

JASMINE

— 43 —

PALESTINE

When I was growing up, even kisses were censored on the television.

The first time I saw kissing on the lips, I asked my mother if she had ever done that with my dad. She said, 'No, no, that's not good, you might catch something.' There was a lot of 'You might catch something' and 'stranger danger', even with myself. Mum and the teachers at school recommended that you get changed as quickly as possible in case you found yourself naked.

I was fifteen or sixteen when I was told by a friend that sex involved the penis going inside the vagina. I was grossed out and lost respect for my mother: *She lets my dad put his disgusting willy inside her body!* There was another wave of that when I learned about blow jobs: *No self respecting woman would do that!*

When I was six, I was briefly kidnapped. The man pulled down my knickers and touched my vulva, then he got nervous and took me home. I wasn't very distressed by it, but I'd been gone for a couple of hours and when I returned, I got all my mum's anger and panic. I think that's been the biggest trauma of my life really.

'Did he touch you?' she asked.

'No.' I was too scared to tell her what he had done.

'Don't ever talk about it again.'

I carried this for a very long time. Now I'm older, I understand my mum's panic; virginity is a big deal and that sort of thing damages a woman's prospects, even a young girl being kidnapped.

I fell in love and got married. We had lots of sex that in my opinion was really shit. It worked for him, it didn't work for me. I thought I was damaged. I'd say, 'Let's go to a sex therapist, maybe there is something they can cure in me.' But he is a Palestinian Muslim like me, he wouldn't do that.

I'd never let him go down on me; I didn't want him to go to my yucky place. He loved blow jobs and I thought *I love him so much, I will do this for him,* but I had a fear of him coming in my mouth, and a very young part of me was thinking, *This is where he pees.* I gave it to him under very strict rules. During the last few years of our marriage, when I loved him less, I even made him wear a condom.

We are divorced now and I don't live in the Middle East anymore.

I have been seeing a part-time lover for four years. I have some blocks around how much I deserve

It feels so, so intimate. I am satisfied. I love loving him.

This might sound a bit crazy or too philosophical, but I feel an element of worship or godliness too, like I am Mother Earth and he is Father Sky. It is heaven.

I have a daughter and I pride myself on how sex- and body-positive

I am resilient and there is a fighter in me. I have broken a chain, and it is magnificent.

love, and, with kids, about how much space I have for a man. Also, I love my dad, and if he gets any hint that I have sex outside marriage he would probably have a heart attack. Sometimes I think I can't be with someone in an official relationship while my dad is alive. It's a grim thought – am I waiting for my dad to die?

With my lover, we have a narrow physical repertoire but it always feels amazing and expansive. We both love penetration; the simpler the better. Missionary is good when my heart is beating with his. Sometimes I say, 'Just stop, do nothing and breathe into my ear.' We do a lot of cuddling before, during and after penetration and a lot of incredibly sensitive gentle stroking.

When he penetrates me, I feel I am not alone. A lot of things drop: I am not my parent's child, I am not my children's parent. All the masks have fallen, and I am just there in my incredible nakedness with him.

we are in our house; she has had her sexual awakening in an environment that really encouraged it. Sad as it was, it was the divorce that facilitated this.

I am resilient and there is a fighter in me. I have broken a chain, and it is magnificent.

Arnelle Woker is an illustrator based in London. She loves to translate the beauty of the female form into curvaceous ladies in the name of body acceptance. ◙ @arnellewoker

It wasn't until my youngest was about two that my body started to get physically turned on again. 'Thank God you came back!'

— MAGGIE

MAGGIE

My husband is away half the time: he's at home for two weeks then at work for two. I feel like what keeps our sex life great is the fact that it's infrequent as a result.

We both know that when he's around and the kids are at school, it will happen.

'Bye, kids!'

'Bye, babies, we love you!'

As soon as the front door closes we are kissing in the hallway. Quite often we have a shower together, give each other a wash and a dry, and then get on to the bed. He usually does a head-to-toe kiss on me. I love kisses on the neck, my chest and then on my breasts and nipples.

We always start with him on top, pretty soft and gentle, taking it slow. He reminded me recently that when we first got together, I said, 'Stop pulling your penis out and slamming it into me, It really hurts.' He said he'd always done that, he'd seen it in porn and thought that was what girls liked.

We used to have flipping-around-the-room sex and I used to love it from behind. Now I can't think of anything worse. Since the kids came along, everything has changed down there. Sex has to be softer and gentler, or it's painful for me, and neither of us want that.

When the kids were little, I could have gone without sex altogether; my body didn't respond sexually at all. I didn't think it would ever come back. The birth of my first child was so traumatic, it went from worse to worse. He was brain-damaged and we ended up suing the hospital as it was human neglect. I also tore from vagina to anus and they overstitched the opening to the vagina. I couldn't have surgery through Medicare to repair it. The doctor said, 'You're better waiting until you have another baby and letting the baby tear it for you.'

It wasn't until my youngest was about two that my body started to get physically turned on again. *Thank God you came back!* I hate that they say you can have sex six weeks after giving birth, it puts so much pressure on the woman. I remember him saying, 'It's been six weeks, are you ready yet?' I was like, 'Fuck no!'

It was also studying to teach yoga that helped me to heal. I learned how to breathe. When we first started having sex again after my son was born, slow, deep breathing and drawn-out sex helped me go from pain to pleasure. Slowing it down and getting out

thinking about what we are going to do for the rest of the day or how my son was upset when he left, then this always brings me back into myself.

We'll go slow and steady with him on top until things heat up and he's nearly going to come. And then I'll go on top. It's not a ten-minute session with me on top or I'd be knackered. I hook my ankles under his calves.

Women should think about sending heart energy down to their base, and men about sending their base energy up to their heart.

of my head and into my body with the help of my breath really helped. But I also had to examine my thoughts and feelings around sex. Sometimes I'd really resent my partner when he wanted it. I found this was because I was jealous; nothing changed for him while my body had gone through so much having our children.

The connection we have through sex carries through to every aspect of our lives together. It was definitely worth working through this. Someone said to me ages ago that, when it comes to sex, women are heart-centric and men base-centric. So women should think about sending heart energy down to their base, and men about sending their base energy up to their heart. I do this by visualizing a green light, going down through yellow then orange and into red. I pull that energy down. If I start to drift away by

He usually squeezes my nipples, and then I'll move his hands to my hips so I can grind more. I am not thinking at this point, just feeling.

I love it when we come at the same time; we normally look at each other. I think we're lucky to have this. This is the only person in the whole wide world that I do this with and I think that's pretty cool.

Sometimes we congratulate ourselves as we lay there hugging afterwards.

'You're so good, babe. Was it good for you? It was good for me.'

'It was awesome.'

The art of Alphachanneling is an holistic exaltation of sexuality. The anonymous artist, based in California, describes their work as 'carnal, explicit and provocative, but in the most gentle, graceful and reverential way'.
🅞 @Alphachanneling

ILLUSTRATION BY ALPHACHANNELING

I haven't really had sex for five years. For a very long time I didn't want anyone touching me at all.

— JENNY

JENNY

I haven't really had sex for five years.

For a very long time I didn't want anyone touching me at all. My ex-husband had always had a slightly abusive side – verbal and a bit physical. It became worse when we had children. One night he had me down on the sofa with my arm behind my back and his hand strangling me. He'd never been that bad before. Something clicked. I called a domestic abuse helpline, and said, 'I know it's not that bad, compared to what some people go through.' The woman at the center said, 'Jenny, this is abuse, it's bad.' From that point I couldn't be loving with him, something had shifted too much.

Then I had an encounter with a girlfriend of mine. She came on to me. It was great. But the repercussions were awful.

So that was two people who'd touched me and I felt betrayed by them both. I didn't want anything to do with anyone in an intimate way after that. I've always enjoyed self-pleasuring so I didn't feel I was missing out.

I remember sitting on the toilet when I was about thirteen and wondering what was inside me. I stuck my fingers in my vagina, and it felt really nice and warm, although I had a feeling that what I was doing was bad, that I was sinning.

If I know I need a sexual release, I'll set my room up nicely with candles and music – not too relaxing though or I will fall asleep. I'll have a shower and give myself a breast massage. When I grew breasts, I felt like I wasn't supposed to have them, as though I was displeasing my parents by becoming a woman. I've got quite big breasts and big nipples, so it was all a bit embarrassing really. Touching them in the shower has changed my view of them. It's really made me enjoy their plump juiciness. They are a bit saggy from breastfeeding my children, but I like that it's part of their story. My nipples feel lovely; I've always liked people touching and sucking them.

I lie naked on my bed, feeling the air, that sensualness which comes from being naked. Sometimes, I'll use my jade egg. I might do an exercise from the Layla Martin jade egg course. You can do weightlifting with your jade egg to get the muscles going. You attach a thread to it servant or subject – a guy, young or old. It used to be the other way round and I was the servant selected by the man of the house to perform. But now I enjoy the power of a queen thinking, *Who will I have today?* Recently I

I get lost, zone out with the feeling of it; I'm in the room but in some kind of pleasure blanket.

and tie on Kegel balls or a little bag of rice. Then you go up on your knees and pull the egg up inside you, which lifts the weight up and down. It's like yoga for the muscles inside your yoni. I went on a Layla Martin retreat in Mexico; there were forty of us doing that, our little rice bags swinging.

I like to gently feel my body down there. I always take my time. I do love my clitoris. A lot of what I do is stimulating my clitoris. I will open the lips and get more intimate with my body. I am usually quite wet, sometimes my fingers get sucked in. I feel inside me; it's always nice and warm there, my little cave. Sometimes I'll pretend I am having sex, with my fingers going in and out, or I might give my G-spot a little tickle.

I get lost, zone out with the feeling of it; I'm in the room but in some kind of pleasure blanket. Or I can be in my fantasy land. Recently my favorite one is where I am a queen, in an amazing palace somewhere hot, and I have all these people at my disposal. I choose someone to come to me. It might be one of my handmaids, or a

have been enjoying fantasising about penises, which shows me I've moved on. I usually fantasize to get me to climax. Afterwards I feel light, alive and whole.

Sex is such a taboo. People get all silly and giggly around it yet. Yet, it's such a fundamental part of who we are. We are sexual beings; this is what we do.

Bárbara Malagoli is a half Italian, half Brazilian illustrator based in London. Her work is all about compositions, shapes, vibrant textures and bold colors. ◙ @bmalagoli

ILLUSTRATION BY BÁRBARA MALAGOLI

MY ORGAS

FROM

I SEE SU

— LING LING

M COMES

NSIDE,

NSHINE.

We have a ritual where I call in the angels and our guides. I'll often ask a question for each of us, and then we take angel cards and get little messages.

— MATYLDA

MATYLDA

Poland is such a Catholic country – even if you aren't part of the church, the tradition remains very strong. It is everywhere you turn.

My parents weren't particularly religious, but for a long time I still had all the hallmarks of a Catholic upbringing deep within me, especially guilt about enjoying sex. I would have sex and feel like a slut. Luckily, I was able to transform this by just being conscious of it.

I know the waves of my libido. After menstruation I feel sexy for two weeks, but then in the last week of my cycle I'm drawn more to soft intimacy, like cuddling. However, two days before my period arrives, I get really horny.

We have a huge living room with a big mattress at the center and not much else. My husband and I go there every night after we put our child to bed.

I like to shower before and then get the space ready by lighting candles and burning Palo Santo or sage. There is a mandala painted on the cover of the mattress, and we sit at the center of it with a little altar. We'll usually be wearing robes.

We have a ritual where I call in the angels and our guides. I'll often ask a question for each of us, and then we take angel cards and get little messages. Then, if we are going to, we sniff rapé. It's a holy tobacco plant from South America. It is really good to clean your energy and get rid of mind-talk after a hectic day. It gives a boost of energy, sometimes very strong, sometimes very relaxing.

We'll embrace and feel the effects, which last for around ten minutes, then we take our robes off and lie down and cuddle. We talk about how we feel, and we also have a ritual where we say three things we love about each other and three things we love about us. It is a very nice introduction, all this conversation deep from the heart really turns me on.

At the beginning, I have my eyes closed, then I alternate between opening and closing my eyes. When I close my eyes I am more with myself and when I open them we are more together. My husband does the same.

When I'm making love I feel beautiful and soft, like there is light and vibration in all parts of my body, and I am larger than my body, more than I am myself. The energy in our bubble is more than we are.

It's very calm. The world doesn't exist; it's as though nothing matters. I never think about my son waking up.

body, and make sensations longer by controlling them. I don't like to come too early. I'm happy that my husband can orgasm without ejaculation, so I know that I can come as many times as I want, and he'll still have energy at a high level.

In my job I help women and couples. It is very often the case that women don't prioritize their sexuality. They have to do everything else first –

It is very often the case that women don't prioritize their sexuality.

Of course, he has woken up, but this is part of life, it doesn't matter.

We don't talk much. We might laugh if we accidently elbow each other. Although, if we have fantasies about another man, woman or threesome, then we'll share these desires – sometimes we do this during penetration.

Yesterday I felt strong sexual energy. My husband asked if he could put his hand on my yoni. He did. There wasn't a lot of action; it was slow motion, very intense, but enough to make me really hot. For me, less is more. I was very much with him as well; feeling his desire made me more turned on. He touched me all over my body. I really like it when he touches my breasts and also my face. I had to stop myself from having an orgasm straight away because I was so turned on.

I wanted to feel him inside me. I like being the one on the top; I can control what is going on with my

serve children, husband, mother-in-law, parents – and because they are so deep in this serving program, it's difficult for them to have sex before they wash the dishes. I try to show them that if they nourish themselves and give time to the strongest energy we have in this life, then they will actually create more time and energy in their life.

Sarah B. Whalen is an illustrator, painter and embroiderer based outside of New York, who specializes in portraits of sex and human intimacy. ⊙ @sarahbwhalen

ILLUSTRATION BY SARAH B. WHALEN

With penetration, there is a relief in my heart. I feel like I have devoured him. 'You're not getting away.'

— REHANA

REHANA

Recently, I was having difficulty having an orgasm. I just felt like I was blocked. But it wasn't about my partner trying something different with my vagina; I could feel that my heart was clenched. I asked him to stroke my chest where my heart is, and as soon as he did that, something shifted in me, and I cried. We talked. The most pleasure I have in sex is when I am connected and open, and connection and openness are about communication, feeling and love, what's happened between you and your partner since you last met or were in bed together, that whole realm.

He and I are in a long-distance relationship; we see each other for short intense periods, and so we spend our time together as though we are on holiday.

I find him very attractive. He's got this kind of life force that is very vibratory, everything in him is so alive. Sometimes just his voice turns me on, it's as if maple syrup had a voice.

I said to him the other night, 'Sometimes when you kiss me you put me in an altered state; within twenty seconds my whole being is softened and I'm out of body as well as in my body.' I can feel a lot of sensation in my womb area, my vagina and my heart. I am open.

With him, there is a 'fire that is about to engulf me' quality about his sexuality and I think, *Do I want to escape and slow down or do I want to let the fire overtake me?* The kisses make me want to have him in me. The gap between the kissing and the sex can be quite small, his hot tip right at the entrance to me, but I slow it down. I love to wait for total hunger, to be at the begging point of 'fuck me now'.

With penetration, there is a relief in my heart. I feel like I have devoured him. *You're not getting away.* It has a still quality. I could have barely moving penetration, enough to keep the cock firm enough for a long time, even an hour, just to keep that feeling of fullness.

When I am really opened, I am

more a sense being and not a thinking being anymore. We are so used to having our awareness in our thinking brain, but in this expanded sensuality, it is more that all sensation is intelligence. Sometimes I describe the sensations to him, and that leads to some playful talk about what is happening.

I surprised him once when I said, 'Right now, the way you are fucking me, it's like a toffee in my mouth has half melted.' He was like, 'What?!' But it was exactly like that: half of my vagina was so molten and full of sweetness, with no edges, and half of it could feel the fullness of his cock.

I love to have my nipples touched and to kiss at the same time. I'm a sensory-overload freak; I would like to have every orifice stuffed and my nipples kissed at the same time. I think the ideal number of lovers would be three at a time – you know, to have enough penises and hands to have all the parts activated. That is my fantasy!

I have seen in porn women rubbing themselves, but if I'm going to bother having sex with someone, I think, *Come on, this is your job!* I will take their hand and lead them to do it. When you're in the throes of the horn, you become a tyrant.

I adore cunnilingus. I think it is one of the most fantastic things on the planet. I like it slow, with pauses and with gentleness. I like to be tou-

People don't have enough time for sex, or for sensuality. Yet every part of the psyche lives in sex.

ched and grabbed, pulled apart a bit and softly stroked. Kiss my knees a bit, kiss my thighs. Meandering cunnilingus, please.

I say 'Oh, God' a lot. It is really interesting that we say 'Oh, God' in sex. It's like the biggest, widest set of beingness that we are trying to speak to because we are in such a state of expanded aliveness.

People don't have enough time for sex, or for sensuality. Yet every part of the psyche lives in sex.

Sabrina Gevaerd is a Brazilian illustrator based in London. She likes to explore the intersection between life and magic, with elements that range from female features to animals.
@sabrinagevaerd

ILLUSTRATION BY SABRINA GEVAERD

For him, it's simple in that if he gets laid, then he thinks we are fine and close, if not, he feels we aren't. Closeness for me isn't just sex, but I have given up trying to be close to him in any other way; now I'm just tired.

— EMMA

EMMA

The attraction for me has gone. Sex is something I am doing for him and not for me anymore.

We have a great friendship and laugh a lot – it's our sense of humor that keeps our relationship going, even in situations that aren't fun – but other than that, I am not sure what else we have. I know he is amazing, I just don't admire him anymore, and we have money issues, which doesn't help.

We have some child-free time at the weekend so that's usually when sex happens. He usually initiates it, not very subtly. He'll be at me, wanting to kiss me in a certain way, or he'll say, 'Give me a kiss.' Urgh, it creeps me out. I'm just like, *Let's do this so he will leave me alone and he off my back*, which is terrible.

I work myself up for it by visualising myself having sex, wondering whether I want a quickie in the shower or if I am up for longer sex. A quickie in the shower will start either with a blow job or naked kissing and caressing. The tricky part is how to get hot water running on both of us.

I like blow jobs; there is something naughty and very sexual about them. It's empowering for me, because I am the one in charge. It becomes hard and I think, *Wow*. It fascinates me. I don't let him do cunnilingus anymore. I find that more intimate than penetration. I don't want to surrender or spend more time than I have to.

When I am done and feel ready for intercourse, I stand up and let him penetrate me. He grabs one of my legs, so I have one leg on the floor and one leg up. Physically we're not twenty anymore and he's not a strong man, so eventually I'll turn around and let him enter me from behind. Normally this happens when it pops out or when I think we might be in danger of breaking our necks. 'How did you die?' 'Well, we were having sex and he dropped me!'

I might focus on how the sensations feel and say, 'Oh, that's good, keep doing that,' but sometimes I'll think of other things, like what I need to do in the backyard.

During penetration I find I can start talking about totally different things, because that's when I have his full attention; there is no phone so he is there with me. There will be a whole list of things, about our life and home,

Sometimes I wonder whether I need a lover to help me re-find my fire. I once met a woman who told me that she paid someone to really give her pleasure. My partner and I did once discuss doing a tantric course,

It's hard to undo something you've been doing for ages. I think if we speak about it then we won't be together anymore, and I am not ready for that.

that I need to say to him, so I do it while we are having intercourse.

It stops when he ejaculates. I don't orgasm but I do enjoy it. I've not generally orgasmed with partners, although I do with clitoris stuff when I self-pleasure. I have never found a way to integrate me touching myself in sex though.

I remember masturbating from eight years old and asking my mum about sex and her being really uncomfortable.

My dad used to cheat on my mum with prostitutes. It was a big drama that my mum would share with me, but not my brothers. And both my brothers would tell me all their sexual stories, even though I was a virgin and much younger than them. Before I was sexually active, there was all this going around me. Then when I was nineteen, I thought, *I need to have sex*, but it was painful.

When I was in my thirties I had a breast lift. I thought, *I am going to experience my new body.*

but if I am honest, I think I need to find myself first, commune with the earth and discover the sacred feminine within me.

For him, it's simple in that if he gets laid, then he thinks we are fine and close, if not, he feels we aren't. Closeness for me isn't just sex, but I have given up trying to be close to him in any other way; now I'm just tired.

It's hard to undo something you've been doing for ages. I think if we speak about it then we won't be together anymore, and I am not ready for that.

Frances Cannon is a queer multidisciplinary artist based in Melbourne, Australia. She works predominantly in drawing and painting in ink, gouache and watercolor. ◉ @frances_cannon

ILLUSTRATION BY FRANCES CANNON

FRANCES
CANNON

I am using his cock. That's what I am doing. I am using his cock for my pleasure. Any pleasure he gets out of that, I am pleased for him, but this is for me.

— ANGELA

ANGELA

I've not had an easy relationship with sex. My first experience of being penetrated was when I raped by three men when I was fifteen. I was meant to go to a U2 concert but I really liked a guy and he was at a party. So I went to the party. He didn't turn up, I got drunk and later I was preyed upon.

A few months later there was a guy who really liked me and wanted to be nice to me. I convinced him we should have sex. We went to this horrible underground car park. There was no lubrication and he didn't know what he was doing. I was trying to force something into something which wasn't ready. It was awful. The next day he didn't talk to me, so I made up a rumor about his cock. I just needed to put something else between me and what happened.

The following year I started seeing a guy. The first time we had sex he ran out of my bedroom halfway through because apparently I was frozen. But I didn't know I was frozen.

I've had some terrible things happen to me. But I am very sexual.

I have a lot of fantasies. I rarely switch them off. In my teens, the fantasies involved Morten Harket, lead singer of a-ha. He was my sexual fantasy man. I imagined I was in an alley and something bad had happened; he found me and was really nice to me, and he was so attracted to me that we ended up kissing and sexual stuff happened. I realize now that it was a coping mechanism as I was traumatized by the rapes.

My coping mechanism now is that I rarely tolerate touch that I don't want. The way I manage that is to ask for things to slow down, or I say that I am not ready.

I went through a phase where I would refuse anything coming into my vagina. I would say, 'Don't enter me, don't even attempt to enter me without asking my explicit permission verbally,' and 'Rather than you fuck me, you stay still and I will fuck you; I will envelop you.'

Then I thought, *Why don't we do that with anal sex?* 'You stay still and I will fuck you with my arse' was a complete game changer. At first, I'm anally stimulated with fingers, mouth, tongue, lips, and then, because I am the one being penetrated, I state when I am ready, and then control to regulate my system and become incredibly relaxed and breathe deeply and open up. I remember once when everything came together: I was lying on my back and he was in

In order to really enjoy anal sex, you have to surrender and you have to trust.

what happens and the depth. The penetration at the beginning is like a rosebud massage, but when you have gone in several inches, that's where the pleasure hits for me. I don't particularly like the coming in and coming out all the time, because my sphincter starts going with all that movement.

The big problem with anal sex is that the person getting penetrated is at the mercy of the person fucking and if they don't know what they are doing – or actually, even if they do know what they are doing – they don't know how you are feeling, or the state of your arse, your sphincter, your diet. You're much more exposed, I think, anally than you are vaginally.

In order to really enjoy anal sex, you have to surrender and you have to trust. You can't fake it because the inner sphincter is a nervous-system response. If you're stressed it will be tight or loose, it will do whatever it wants to do.

'I want you in and I want you to stay in, that's what I want.'

I am the one moving, changing the pace, depth and intensity. I am able

me anally; I had my Magic Wand on my lips and my mons and my clit. I was loving not having his bloody cock or part of his body knocking my wand out of the way.

I am using his cock. That's what I am doing. I am using his cock for my pleasure. Any pleasure he gets out of that, I am pleased for him, but this is for me. It's really healthy taking. I think the majority of women rarely experience that and it pisses me off that they don't.

Jasmine Chin is an award-winning illustrator based in London. She creates playful and quirky illustrations inspired by popular culture.
🅞 @this_is_jasmine_chin

My rabbit is really nice. When the battery is full it's really quick – brrrrrrrr – and my orgasm comes like a huge explosion.

— MARIA

MARIA

— 50 —

SPAIN

I didn't enjoy sex until I was thirty-five years old and met my husband. Our sexual relationship was amazing, but then eight years ago I got cancer.

When you're told you have cancer, your life changes completely. I had a six-year-old boy so I told my surgeon, 'Cut everything you need to cut, just keep me alive, because I need to see my son become a man.' I had a full mastectomy, chemotherapy and radiotherapy. Your body and spirit become more and more exhausted. I tried to get my energy back and smile and cuddle, but I wasn't able to do much sex. Since then I've had years of medication, which has brought my sex drive right down.

Now, our sexual relationship is almost at zero; we do it maybe once every six months or once a year.

I feel really sorry for my husband; he's a perfectly healthy fifty-two-year-old man and obviously he wants to be with me sexually. He tries to make me feel in the mood, saying how beautiful I and my body are. I feel really stressed when that happens.

He wants me to react to his words and feelings, but I am not reacting – on the contrary, I'm making thousands of excuses. It makes me feel depressed and like I'm failing him.

However, it happened this morning.

I'd been dreaming about having sex with him. I didn't know it was him at first; I was in a house with a man, I couldn't see his face, but he was very grumpy. We were arguing in the kitchen and he said, 'Don't you realize that I don't know how to approach you, and that I am in love with you,' He started kissing me, I saw it was him. Then we had tender sex.

I was waking up, halfway in and out of this dream, and cuddling my husband in real life. I looked at him cheekily, then he looked at me as though to ask, 'Is this going to be my lucky day?'

He was very gentle. He didn't use to be so gentle, before he was more fire. I like kissing him and the way he touches me all over. It doesn't matter what part of my body he touches, he always makes my hair stand up.

I love the way he caresses my breasts. Some people might be put off when they see women's breasts after having had a mastectomy, but he's not like that. He makes me feel like it doesn't matter how my body is, that he will experience the same with or

got out our rabbit vibrator to help me.

My rabbit is really nice. When the battery is full it's really quick – *brrrrrrrr* – and my orgasm comes like a huge explosion. My husband is very naughty, he keeps it there, and

You feel different after sex. There's a closeness which carries on all day long.

without my breasts, and I am capable to achieve the same with or without my breasts.

I really like my clitoris being touched. However, I don't enjoy his fingers in my vagina. The only thing I can bear and enjoy inside my vagina is his penis. I don't know whether that's because of what happened when I was a child.

I was raped by my uncle when I was thirteen. He was driving me somewhere, then he parked up and all of a sudden he had his hands and breath all over me. When I told my mum, she said I was lying, and there was nothing I could say for her to believe me. It was the worst moment in my life. That was thirty-seven years ago and I haven't been able to overcome it. Every time it comes into my head, I have to try to think of positive things in my life to try and change my mood.

Because we don't have a sexual relationship anymore, this morning when we did it after my dream, my husband finished early, but then he

then I get another one and another. One day I lost my voice because of all the orgasms and excitement; they kept coming like they couldn't stop, it was so amazing. I love my rabbit.

You feel different after sex. There's a closeness which carries on all day long. This morning, the way we looked at each other was so connected because we'd been exposed entirely to each other. I felt complete with him, like a whole round thing, a little bubble jumping, 'I'm so happy, I'm so happy.'

Nikki Peck is an artist living and working in Vancouver, BC. Placing the feminine queer gaze at the forefront, Peck examines under what conditions the act of drawing (specifically with graphite and ink) can empower female sexuality in today's society. ◙ @ bonercandy69

ILLUSTRATION BY NIKKI PECK

I think I take really cool sensual artistic pictures and then he comes back with his cock in the middle of the screen, like BOOM.

— TEREZA

TEREZA

I'm married, but we're in a crisis at the moment.

I used to like how my husband came towards me sexually, how his hands would very gently touch my body, and he always made sure that I had pleasure.

But if I tried to initiate, he'd say, 'No, no,' or 'Don't push me.' I had to wait for him to show interest, which I thought was a bit sexist. But then he stopped coming on to me in that way. I'm not sure why, maybe because he smokes a lot of marijuana, but also, I think he started to feel disappointed in me somehow and it turned him off me. He constantly criticized me instead.

I said to him, 'It's getting hard for me. It's not that I want other people, but since I don't have you, what am I going to do?' I feel very loyal to my partner but at the same time I need sex. Sex is like having a meal and I am hungry! He became upset, while I became obsessed with my unmet sexual needs. We drifted apart and now we sleep in separate rooms.

Some months ago, an old friend contacted me over the internet and said he'd had a crush on me for thirty years. He is married too, we haven't met, but we have been sending pictures to each other.

I've never in my life made sensual pictures of myself, but I've discovered it makes me feel very sexy. I've been buying new lingerie – I might show him a bit of bra and cleavage, or take some photos of me in the bathtub. I took some pictures of my shadow once which looked wonderful. Each time I'll try to change the theme and the lingerie.

I think I take really cool sensual artistic pictures and then he comes back with his cock in the middle of the screen, like BOOM. Or he says, 'I want to see your lips.' A man and a lady's minds are in completely different places. This man just wants to see my hole! I think women need more fantasy, courtesy, flowers. Even if they are virtual flowers.

He recently sent me a porn film. I watched it, of course, and it did make me feel hot, but at the same time it was a film that had no feeling in it. We had a virtual sexual encounter that evening but the next morning, I seen women humiliate themselves with married men and I don't want that.

These could be my last sexual years; I know that as women get older

It has been thirty years and I have only been with one person. I feel like I am a virgin again.

thought, *Why is he sending me these things, does he want me to be his bitch?!*

We masturbate during our exchanges, while texting and taking pictures of ourselves with the other hand. I take them on my camera roll, choose the best one and send it via Instagram messenger. But then seconds later I delete it.

We always aim to come together. When I tell him that I came, he says, 'Okay, bye-bye!' I think, *Oh, that's the kind of guy you are, the kind who gets what he wants.* I guess he has to run back to his wife and his bedroom. And after about three days I hear from him again. That's the pattern.

This morning I thought, *I'm going to send a message and say goodbye, never more, don't contact me again,* but I couldn't do it. He is just focused on sex and I maybe wish he could be more interested in me and who I am.

I don't think we should meet for real – I don't want to disturb his life – but then I wonder whether we should have one encounter to experience before cutting it off. Although I'm not sure if I'd be able to do that then; I'm afraid of how involved I would get. I've

they start to feel dry and not have so much libido. I feel like I am having my last moment, and I have to take it and enjoy it! I am in this beautiful body! Having all these excitements and I don't want to lose this!

It has been thirty years and I have only been with one person. I feel like I am a virgin again.

Destiny Darcel is an artist based in Atlanta. She currently balances working as a software engineer, designer and illustrator, focusing on celebrating black women. ◉ @destinydarcel

ILLUSTRATION BY DESTINY DARCEL

fore

play

The story I come back to often is a fantasy where the main character is a former fiancée of a wizard. She is also a succubi, a female demon who feeds off sex. He is a master of a harem called the House of Joy. They meet a lesbian elf maiden and have a lot of sex.

— LILY

LILY

– 50 –

SWEDEN

Sometimes I go without masturbating for weeks, sometimes I do it five times in a day. I use it to stop thinking, like when I practise mindfulness. I use it as a way to connect with myself.

Six months ago I discovered that I can ejaculate. It's really messy, but fun. I got this new toy, an air tickler for clitoral stimulation. It looks like something you would have in your bathroom or kitchen, but I've never had anything like it, it's 'less than a minute' efficient. With a partner, I think sex is really good if you take your time, but I just want to get on with it if I'm on my own.

I lock the door because you never know what my mother, who lives nearby, might do. I fold a towel into four or five folds and lie in the bed under the cover. I might be naked down below. I'll have my iPad. My dog will get up on to the bed, he always does. I read for a bit to get in the mood; I adore erotic cartoons and novels.

I don't like porn, for justice reasons. I've taught civics, politics, soci-ology and economics – every Swedish kid takes it up until they graduate. I saw a site called The Truth About Porn; they have two-minute interviews with all kinds of people affected by porn. About five years ago I understood how much porn relies on trafficked victims. Now, it doesn't turn me on. But cartoons are a completely different story.

You have to do a bit of research because even cartoon sex has a bit of misogyny, and the Japanese ones where the characters look like children are not right. I like cartoons with active women who participate. The story I come back to often is a fantasy where the main character is a former fiancée of a wizard. She is also a succubi, a female demon who feeds off sex. He is a master of a harem called the House of Joy. They meet a lesbian elf maiden and have a lot of sex.

I'll read for a while and then turn the thing on. My head will be in the story to start with but after a while, sensations will take over.

I think I'm more orgasmic as I am

older. I know my body better. I look back on my youth and think, *Why didn't I do this? Why didn't I do that?* I was so sensitive back then; I wanted to look good, it wasn't about the sex at all. Now, I don't care.

On about orgasm number three I get a tickle feeling under the clitoris.

sex, I kind of forced him into it. I had bought a vibrating, blinking, plastic cock ring. It was a fun toy, and he came in three seconds. I was so disappointed – normally he would take care of me and do stuff, but now he just wanted me off him.

I think if a man had done this to

I am me-sexual now, but I would like to be someone-else-sexual. It's a sorrow I have.

When that happens, I push out, like I would when I pee. It's an odorless liquid that feels like it comes from glands that fill up. It's very different from a normal orgasm; it goes all the way up to my brain. After a normal orgasm I can get up and go, but with this I have to collect myself. I stay quiet for a few minutes breathing; I won't have thoughts.

I am aware that with my last boyfriend, when intimacy disappeared from our relationship, I tried to exchange it for sex. I didn't want sex but I needed a way to communicate intimately with him. I carry that trauma with me now.

His marriage had broken apart. When his kids were small, his wife stopped wanting sex. He was obviously feeling rejected, as someone who wanted to feel seen and heard and loved. But that's not how he expressed it – he said that as long as he got sex, he was happy. But it turned out that wasn't the case at all.

I remember the last time we had

a woman, it would have been rape. I think I raped him. It was awful. That was six years ago. I think about it quite a lot.

I am me-sexual now, but I would like to be someone-else-sexual. It's a sorrow I have.

Kate Philipson is a freelance graphic illustrator from London. Her illustrations have a strong feminine style with bold lines and colors that burst. She is inspired by popular culture, fashion photography and graphic novels.
@leopardslunch

ILLUSTRATION BY KATE PHILIPSON

Orgasm used to be really, really important to me, but it isn't so anymore. I'd be happy to self-pleasure a few times a month.

— DEARBHLA

DEARBHLA

– 53 –

IRELAND

Our house is a rental, and they've done nothing to it in forty years. I know I am so lucky to have a house to live in, but I walk into that bedroom and it's like a contraceptive, it's so fucking ugly. Plus the walls are thin, there's an echo, and we have the kids in the house, so they can hear every thing if we're not careful.

I am the only woman. I have a partner and two sons; we even have a male dog. I keep the whole house together – shopping, cooking, laundry, house cleaning.

We probably have sex once or twice a month, but I could go from one end of the month to the other without it. I want a happy and active sex life but I've become angry and resentful at the fact it's me who has to make the effort. I'm tired. Orgasm used to be really, really important to me, but it isn't so anymore. I'd be happy to self-pleasure a few times a month.

I love my partner, he's a phenomenal guy, and we get on really well. Thankfully I don't feel pressured by

him to have sex. He's sensitive – he waits for an opportunity to connect with me, and when I am open to it, he is utterly there to meet me.

We had a breakthrough last Friday and I'm really glad about that. I had done an hour of meditation on my own and afterwards I felt wonderful – calm and expanded. I went downstairs and said to him, 'It might be nice to make love tonight.'

He came upstairs, we got naked and he asked, 'Should we do a plug-in?' This is what we call it when he puts his lingam – this is the tantric word for penis – in me and we don't really move much.

I actually realized that my language with him at times can be quite violent – sometimes I snap – but this time I really softened my words, and said, 'I'm not ready for that, but what I would like is for you to put your hand on my yoni.' At first, explaining what I wanted took me away from my experience, but I carried on and asked him for a lighter touch, until his hand was almost hovering there. I am very sensitive to touch and energy; if his hand hovers a few inches above my skin, I feel something.

He was very intuitive and started to move his hands up my body; it felt

thing he loves but I have totally gone off. For me it feels like I am giving, and I give so much in a day. But that day I wanted to. Then I took his lingam in my hands, and then into my mouth;

A friend and I have just set up a women's circle, so we can all support and inspire each other to have gourmet sex and fulfillling, intimate lives.

good. He caressed my breasts, he sucked my nipples; it was amazing. Then we did go for a plug-in.

I stimulated my own clitoris while he gently moved in me. When we first got together, we studied tantra together for years, and recently I've been listening to a sex therapist called Kim Anami. I've learned how, rather than go straight for an orgasm, I can hover in an orgasmic state for some time, edging upwards, so that the climax, when I do have it, is even greater. When I get to seven on a scale of one to ten, with ten being climax, I will plateau there for a while by controlling my breathing. I breathe in for the count of four, hold for four and then release for six. I creep my arousal up in little chunks. It can get to the point where we don't know which is the yoni, which is the lingam.

Back in the room last Friday, I had an orgasm that was nice, but not earth-shattering; sometimes the journey is better than the destination. After a few minutes of basking, I wanted to kiss him, which is some-

it really felt right for me to swallow, which is something I do rarely.

He said to me the next evening, 'I'm still buzzing from last night.'

Talking about my sexuality for this book has been a big experience for me; I've realized I want this sort of gourmet sex, and I'm willing to put the work in to get it. But I want to do it with a tribe of women. A friend and I have just set up a women's circle, so we can all support and inspire each other to have gourmet sex and fulfillling, intimate lives.

Cris Ruiz is an artist based in Barcelona. She specializes in wall art posters from the late 60s psychedelic movement that celebrate sexual liberation. ◉ @ goldendaze_illustration

ILLUSTRATION BY GOLDEN DAZE ILLUSTRATION

Most people are shocked that I am willing to talk about sex and domestic violence so openly. We are still so dominated by what people will think.

— ANITA

ANITA

INDIA

I'm divorced.

It wasn't a great sexual relationship with my husband. He was really quick, in and out. We live in the land of the bloody Kama Sutra with its 108 positions and we didn't try any of them!

He didn't mind oral sex as long as I did it to him. I don't think Indian men know how to do oral sex. They end up bruising you or hurting you and they don't get the spot. It's a waste of time, especially because you're supposed to be indebted to them if they do it.

I was once in a relationship for four years and I asked my boyfriend why he didn't go down on me. He said, 'It's not clean, it's your urinary tract.' I said, 'What about your fuck ing urinary tract?!'

I am a bit of a rebel. My father died when I was really young and then I was sent to boarding school. I was sexually abused when I was nine. The guy couldn't penetrate me because I think he was inexperienced but it's still a very shocking experience for a young girl to go through.

Most Indian people just brush this under the carpet. I've spoken to many friends, including male friends, who have been similarly abused and the adults didn't want to hear about it. I was a very angry person as a teenager, maybe because of these things that shaped me.

I was married at fifteen to a man who was twenty years older than me. The first time we had proper sex with penetration I was scared about how painful it would be. We girls were so innocent, we had no idea we were supposed to experience pleasure.

One of the reasons I left him was that he used to hit me. He wouldn't deliberately hurt me during sex but if he found I was in discomfort it excited him. He liked it rough.

I first experienced pleasure during sex when I got on top of him for the first time. It was the most amazing feeling. I didn't know anyone could feel like that. It was like a tingle all over, an electric shock, where you feel all your fingers and toes. Complete bliss. I wanted it all the time!

Many times he did let me go on top but often he wanted to assert himself so he would go on top.

India is a very male-dominated society; it has repressed women. We're not meant to have urges and we are certainly not meant to want to have an orgasm.

I have explored my pleasure. I know what I like, but you have to find the right partner. I like kissing,

3. And teach her what you like!

I had a boyfriend – let's call him Mr A – who liked to be penetrated in his anus with a finger. He didn't know how to go down on me either, but I felt so much pleasure that I was able to excite him to such a pitch.

Most people are shocked that I am willing to talk about sex and domestic violence so openly. We are still so dominated by what people will

India is a very male-dominated society; it has repressed women. We're not meant to have urges and we are certainly not meant to want to have an orgasm.

although it depends on whether he knows what he is doing. I don't like spittle! Or teeth clashing! My favorite areas to be touched are the nape and side of the neck, my ears and my nipples. I like to have my nipples touched or even sucked, and my clitoris.

If I can trust that he knows what he's doing, then I don't mind him going down on me. I like it when we are both performing oral sex at the same time, that in itself is a turn-on. I'm on top of him, my head in-between his legs and his head in-between my legs.

If I had to give sex advice to Indian men, I would say:
1. Slow down – be a bit gentle, go a bit slow.
2. Get to know a woman's body – ask her what she likes, it doesn't make you less of a man.

think. Certainly this has ruled my life. Even now my mother still says, 'What will the neighbors say?' I reply, 'Do they pay the bills?'

It is changing, though, women are becoming more bold and learning to assert themselves.

Anshika 'Ash' Khullar is an Indian, non-binary transgender illustrator based in Southampton, England. Their art focuses on intersectional feminist narratives, with the aim of showcasing the ordinary as beautiful. @ @aorists

ILLUSTRATION BY ANSHIKA 'ASH' KHULLAR

Basically, bad sex is not worth it anymore. It's too much hassle; why the fuck bother?

— ODILE

ODILE

'Let's go into the Temple.'

When he says it, it's very matter-of-fact, but inside I'm thinking, *Yippee!*

We have a temple shed in the garden, a scared space. The deities that we work with are very present there. His are Buddhist yidam deities and I work mainly with the goddess Rhiannon and the Horned God. We take our shoes off, light candles and incense, then we get undressed. We may go there specifically to do certain practices or we could just meet there as lovers.

If we meet as lovers, we do a visualization. 'Our deities are here, the elemental beings are here, the ancestors are here, the great guides are here,' and then we start lovemaking. It is a form of prayer.

Patriarchal religions have made sex sinful, highly taboo or restrictive, whereas the pagan path, and particularly the goddess path, is far more centered around the sacredness of sexuality and the body.

I might do a tantric ceremony where I raise sexual energy in my body, sensual movement of the bowl of the pelvis, then I breathe into the yoni, the clitoris, the inner parts of the yoni, up to the moon gateway of the cervix, into the womb space. I visualize the temple space of my body, preparing it for the arrival of the god in the form of the lingam, the magic wand.

Or we can do a breath circle together, a very basic but very beautiful tantric practice to circulate energy. Breathing energy into the yoni, then up to the womb, and then to the heart, out of the heart into his heart down to the lingam out of the lingam into the yoni.

He has a beautiful cock. And I love it everywhere. I love opening to a man. I love being penetrated by the loving presence that is the cock of the beloved. It is so goddam gorgeous. I don't know why it is not talked about more in these delicious terms.

Because my body is changing, sometimes energetically I am there, but physically I am not as wet as I was in the past. We use what we call 'joy juice', some nice lubricant, so that it's smooth and easy. It's not an issue. It's an anointing.

We can have really energetic lovemaking, but often it's very subtle with not a lot of movement. We allow the sexual energy to move in our bodies, surrendering to it rather than doing anything. This doesn't mean we lie

waves that can keep going for a very long time.

The menopause has been a big gateway. I had been very in tune with my body, my moon cycles and my fertility, since my mid-teens, then the crone says, 'Do you want a deeper wisdom? Then you have to unlearn everything you've ever learned.' You

The menopause has been a big gateway … You own your body now; it's not for other things anymore.

there like corpses; I make a lot of sound and my body might tremble.

There is no goal. It's a practice of not thinking, just being, and of not being separate from each other. It's an expansion and I love that. Of course, things take you out of it – if I fart or something – but so what, you just have a giggle and carry on. It's not so serious.

I love having him inside me. If I go into my softness, the soft power of the feminine, my entire body is orgasmic; we have so many erogenous zones. But it is less a 'getting to' and more a 'relaxing into', an arriving into something that already is, which you make more alive within you.

For me, clitoris orgasms are wonderful, entry to the yoni temple is wonderful, goddess-spot orgasms are wonderful, awe-inspiring. A-spot orgasms are wonderful; full body, nipples, armpits, wrists, palms of the hands, sides of the neck, mouth, and eye orgasms are wonderful. Oceanic

own your body now; it's not for other things anymore. It's not for babies, or to please the distorted masculine in our society with our youth because that has gone.

I don't like that I am less horny and turned on than I used to be, but I think that while the intensity of sexual energy is less, the glow is more. It is subtler and when it does rise, it is very sweet.

Basically, bad sex is not worth it anymore. It's too much hassle; why the fuck bother?

Sabrina Gevaerd is a Brazilian illustrator based in London. She likes to explore the intersection between life and magic, with elements that range from female features to animals.
⊙ @sabrinagevaerd

ILLUSTRATION BY SABRINA GEVAERD

*When I first lived
with a man, I made
him a boiled egg salad.
I peeled the eggs, and
then placed them in my
vagina before serving
him the salad. I never
told him I had done
that, and I got such
a kick from watching
him eat it.*

— ANJA

ANJA

I want a real Dom.

I am not submissive to anybody, but I am submissive to those who know how to appreciate my submissiveness. The devotion of a woman or man is a very special gift.

If I meet someone and we go to a beer garden, I won't say anything. I wait. I want him to say, 'Okay, we'll go to this corner,' and 'I want to sit here, you go there.' He could even say, 'Go to the bathroom, take off your panties if you have them on, and sit without panties,' and I would do it. That would be very arousing to me.

BDSM is a state of mind, a bond between the Dom and the submissive. It is an interaction of wisdom and well being, a secret together that others don't know about. We don't have to do much; it's about the attention I get and the attention I give him, in being ready for his wishes. This is like a cocoon for me; I feel protected and that's a very beautiful feeling.

My ex-partner and I would rent a studio room with BDSM furniture for four hours. In BDSM when you play for four hours, it feels like half an hour.

One session sticks in my mind. He blindfolded me and tied me up with my arms above my head and my legs spread out. He put out his equipment after I was blindfolded so I didn't know what was going on. My senses being taken away made my feelings more intense. He put clothes pegs on my nipples, which are so sensitive anyway. I was frightened because I didn't know what he would do next, and because I knew he was a Dominant-sadist. He had told me that BDSM was his opportunity to let the monster out and live his aggressions in a so-called accepted form of brutality. That's quite edgy. Maybe it brought something up that I was already feeling about him. There was nobody else nearby; I was completely alone if anything happened against my will.

I started screaming. Blank fear. Woah.

He was shocked that I was scared. We'd never had that before. He held me. He calmed me down. 'Breathe, we'll have a break.'

When we carried on, he beat me with a hand on the arse. I love this, it's intimate and precise. Pure sensation and arousal though pain. A strong caress. *Bam.* I love the beautiful spanking sound, full and sexy. The arse gets hot. The hand stays in

ents were chronically sick. It was very depressing for me sometimes. War bullshit. Traumatized parents and grandparents.

I was taught nothing about sex so I went to the library when I was fourteen and read everything I could. I started with Masters and Johnson's texts. It gave me a scientific way to understand

I mostly find people who are not into BDSM boring; they aren't sexy or open enough for me.

contact for a moment and the impact wave goes through the whole body. It can really hurt, especially if it's for a long time on the same spot, and I can start crying.

Spanking is the warming-up phase, so I felt a lot of anticipation for what would come next.

He put me over a box, exposing my arse again. He put his leg between mine to make me spread out. This is a very sexy move. It says, do what I want. Then he used a flogger. At one point he told me to change position. I was so submissive that I felt as though I was in bondage, that I couldn't move an inch from where he put me. Most of the time in these sessions I don't think, but then I had the thought, *Shit, this is heavy stuff today. I am really under his control.* I was amazed at the power.

I was fifty when I started to think, *What do I like? What are my preferences?*

I grew up in a tense environment. My childhood wasn't easy as my par-

sexuality that was fascinating.

I used to urinate on the living room floor; it aroused me and doing something forbidden and different gave me a feeling of freedom. I think this was the start of my BDSM. And I remember when I first lived with a man, I made him a boiled egg salad. I peeled the eggs, and then placed them in my vagina before serving him the salad. I never told him I had done that, and I got such a kick from watching him eat it.

Sexuality-wise I mostly find people who are not into BDSM boring; they aren't sexy or open enough for me and they're not in contact with their own sexual power and energy.

I think people need to know that female sexuality is for real.

Miranda Lorikeet is a Sydney-based illustrator who draws naked women, landscapes and still-life paintings purely with Microsoft Paint.
 @mirandalorikeet

ILLUSTRATION BY MIRANDA LORIKEET

*It was very important
for a guy to give me some
love and attention, and
sex was one way for me
to have that. Now I'm
more conscious of this,
I ask, 'What is this hole
I am feeling?'*

— JOY

JOY

Sex for my husband and I used to be very important. He says he was a virgin until he met me, I was so good at it! But three years ago I was operated on and since then it's been difficult.

One of the operations was in the vagina; the wall between my vagina and my rectum was cut because the tissue was damaged and poop was leaking inside my vagina. It was very painful for a year afterwards. Even now it's not like it was, so I think I unconsciously block the feelings for sex.

He had prostate cancer too and was treated with radiotherapy. I began to be afraid of the radiation. I spoke to the doctor who said it wasn't a problem, but it was in my head. He doesn't have sperm now. Something comes out, but it doesn't taste or smell the same.

He always wants sex with me. We have it two or three times a week, but if it was down to me I would have sex once a fortnight. I love him and I don't see my life without him, but now if he comes towards me and touches

me because he wants sex, I think, *Oh God*. I'll try to say, 'I'm not feeling well,' or I pretend I'm too tired. Sometimes he thinks I don't like him anymore, but that's not true, it's only my body that doesn't want to do it.

He understands but sometimes the man thinks with the penis. The penis is very important. When he had cancer, he said to the doctor, I don't want to live if I can't have sex. And he is sixty-nine. I feel that in Portugal, guys think they are men because they have a penis.

Sometimes I want to, or I don't mind. We go quickly towards penetration. It's not a problem for me, I am always wet. I have seven hernias so I can't be on my back with him over me. We always do it like I'm a dog, but he doesn't like that so much; he wants to be looking at me. But I can't do that because I am in so much pain.

I touch my clitoris during sex. Before I used to be able to have one, two, three clitoral orgasms, every time, it was very easy. Now it's more difficult; I don't know whether I need to take some hormones.

I have always had fantasies, both during masturbation and sex. I tend to have a fantasy where two guys are making love in front of me. They are having oral and anal sex with each other. Once, a long time ago, I saw a nice movie on television and it was about a love between two guys. It wasn't a porno, you didn't really

very far away; his relationship with my mother wasn't very good and we had a lot of fear towards him. It was very important for a guy to give me some love and attention, and sex was one way for me to have that. Now I'm more conscious of this, I ask, *What is this hole I am feeling?*

I tend to have a fantasy where two guys are making love in front of me.

see anything sexual, but you did see them kiss in the bath. It's stayed in my head. I think homosexuality between two men is beautiful. The best bit of the fantasy for me is that moment when one puts his penis in the other. I used to have a fantasy where I was on a table and there were ten guys around me, kissing me, touching me and having sex with me. Not now. One is enough!

Before, sex would last an hour, now it'll take five or ten minutes. The more we women scream, the quicker they come. I don't feel bad afterwards like I used to with my first husband. In that marriage there was domestic violence. For the last three years I didn't want sex. I was raped; he said it was my duty. It was very intense. My body closed and I had a lot of pain. Now I'm married to someone else, and he respects me, but the duty feeling is still there sometimes.

I think in my early life, I used to have a lot of sex because I needed love and attention. My father was always

Frances Cannon is a queer multidisciplinary artist based in Melbourne, Australia. She works predominantly in drawing and painting in ink, gouache and watercolor. @frances_cannon

ILLUSTRATION BY FRANCES CANNON

I WANT

I WANT

I WA

— VIVIAN

WHAT

WHEN

NT IT

My desire might be a bit less than it was before, but I'm still very sexual, especially if I have a few drinks. I think about sex, watch porn and have a wonderful vibrator.

— CORAL

CORAL

CANADA

I've had some really weird-ass lovers. My last one had no control, he would just pump and dump.

I said to him once, 'Man, you've gotta jerk off, you've gotta practice that shit. You can press next to your balls.'

I think he was embarrassed that he didn't know about this stuff, so he got some Viagra from his doctor. He'd take half a caplet because it's quite expensive, forty dollars for eight pills, but Viagra is better if the man doesn't have other health issues, and this guy was diabetic type 2; he had high cholesterol and was on meds already. The Viagra gave him a permanent red flush and heart palpitations. He'd be exhausted after sex, and not look so good.

He thought that if he could get a better and longer hard-on he would be able to satisfy me. What he didn't realize was that I'm more into the lead-up to sex. I like to be touched. I'd say to him, 'Run your hand across my shoulder, hold my hand, that fills my tank, you don't have to be screwing me to turn me on.' But he didn't listen; he didn't care.

I'd arrive after an hour and a half of driving and he'd be straight to kissing and massaging my boobs. I'd say, 'Can I at least go to the bathroom and have a drink first?' Even then he would be looking at my breasts and getting grumbly.

He liked my boobs. I'm a 38D and they're still quite firm. I never had little sucklings, so for a man to be on my breasts it's purely sexual as I've never had that nursing feeling. He wasn't so good at touching them though. I'd often say: 'They are quite tender, think of them as your balls, not rubber ones.'

He didn't like cunnilingus. He said he was an atheist, but I think there was still Catholicism there holding him back from experimenting and expressing himself. There was always tons of oral sex from me. I liked turning him on, to me it was like licking a lollipop! I would always be hoping I would get the favor in return or at least some verbal reassurance as to just how much he was enjoying it, but all he would ever say is, 'Oh, it's all good.'

He would try to enter but I always wanted to be more aroused. I'd tell him I wasn't ready and he would get

orgasm, unless I was a bit loaded with a marijuana brownie and very relaxed.

Talk about a displeased lover. Afterwards he would fall asleep and I would get up, thinking, *Fuck*. I'd

This man broke my spirit and I'm only just getting myself together again now.

the lube, instead of trying to make me wet himself. It really wasn't very romantic. In my head I'd be asking myself why I was still doing this.

Since the menopause, I have problems with atrophy. I'm very dry, although if it's well lubed, it's not too bad. The atrophy also affects women when they have a pee: the lips curl in and you pee on your leg and all over yourself. It's old lady shit and I hate it. I also got belly weight gain so I'm not so comfortable being naked, and I used to love being naked. My left nipple has lost sensation too; I feel far more in my right. My desire might be a bit less than it was before, but I'm still very sexual, especially if I have a few drinks. I think about sex, watch porn and have a wonderful vibrator.

I love the smell and the weight of a man though, and you don't get that with the vibrator. I like penetration, him on top of me, or me on the edge of the bed, or me sitting on him. With my ex, if I could tell he was about to come, I'd change position to slow things down a bit and see if I could satisfy myself. I would very rarely

be so disappointed: disappointed that I wasn't satisfied, disappointed in myself for putting myself in that position, disappointed that I'd just repeated history again. I let him treat me like that, it wasn't only his fault.

This man broke my spirit and I'm only just getting myself together again now.

Bárbara Malagoli is a half Italian, half Brazilian illustrator based in London. Her work is all about compositions, shapes, vibrant textures and bold colors. ⊙ @bmalagoli

ILLUSTRATION BY BÁRBARA MALAGOLI

I think women are stronger than most men. Men don't have friends like women have friends so when men meet someone, they want you to be their everything.

— VIVIAN

VIVIAN

– 70 –

USA

I want what I want when I want it.

I used to meet men in bars. I had my wild days, before AIDS happened, when I would leave a bar with two guys. Now I do online dating, but I'm not going to spend a lot of time texting back and forth. You read a text in the voice you want to hear, not the voice it might have been written in. It's best to get straight to it: 'Let's meet or not meet.'

If they put in their profile, 'I just want that one last love,' I think, *Oh my God, well it certainly is not going to be me!* To me that sounds like, 'I need to be taken care of, I want someone to make my bed, cook for me and do my laundry.'

I don't want a husband. I don't even think I want to spend a whole weekend with someone. Now I am wondering about an ex-boyfriend and if maybe we could do friends with benefits.

I think women are stronger than most men. Men don't have friends like women have friends so when men meet someone, they want you to be their everything.

Men are very intimidated by me at the beginning. I don't beat about the bush – what's the point, we don't have much time left. When I start dating somebody, I probably sleep with him before most women my age would. I'd never hook up on the first date, but I don't have to wait for anything, not the engagement ring, or the fourth dinner.

I find that I have way more sex drive than most men my age and that is sort of unsatisfying. Men at this age are tired all the time. I am like, 'What? You've done nothing all day. I've mowed the back forty!' Also, more and more, they can't maintain their erection. I am always very compassionate about it, but they're mortified so you can't dwell on it, unless you are really mean.

We don't have wild sex all over the house anymore; most men are too refined or afraid of that. It all happens in bed. Sometimes I say, 'I want sex,' or I just jump on top of them. If I am on top of someone and they don't want it, I keep at it until I get what I want. I joke around, get them laughing and eventually they give in. Then I grab their penis or try and give them a blow job.

I think in general most people want sex; as long as you keep it fresh and exciting, you don't have to do too much persuading. If I really get the

about why I will never do it with this person again.

After sex, if I've got everything I want, I am relaxed and ready to go to sleep. I can say, 'Okay, go to sleep, thanks, see you in the morning. Be ready!'

I like to have sex in the morning too.

I like different positions for penetration. But that becomes harder as you get older, with your joints.

point that they are not interested, then I accept it, and get them to hold me or cuddle me instead.

There are different times when I like different things; giving oral sex depends on the mood I am in at that moment. Sometimes I don't want anyone touching my breasts or smacking my butt, but then other times I ask for that. I enjoy receiving oral sex, but after a while I think, *That's enough, let's do something else now. Don't bore me!* Most of all, I don't want things to become routine.

I like different positions for penetration. But that becomes harder as you get older, with your joints. Oh, my knees! I like to be on top or them on top, and I like it from behind. I used to have anal sex, which I enjoyed, but I would always get a bladder infection afterwards. After the third or fourth time, I thought, *I'm not doing that anymore.*

If I'm thinking about something besides the sex I am having at that moment, then I am probably thinking

The ideal changes as you get older. Years ago I thought the ideal was to be in love. Now I just want what I want when I want it.

Jenny Eclair is a stand-up comic and bestselling writer. In her spare time she paints with acrylics.
🐦 @jennyeclair

ILLUSTRATION BY JENNY ECLAIR

We were married for thirteen years, until I found out about his affairs. When we divorced, I was only hit on by married men. Welcome to the world.

— LUCY

LUCY

I can bring to mind many moments of my fulfillling sex life and of feeling loved. How wonderful is that? I'll be walking down the street and I'll think of this person and get a nice warm sensation.

Sometimes I masturbate if I want to feel special. I think of it as looking after myself; it's better than going with someone I don't really want to go with. It's quite erratic – I may be feeling a bit alone, or think it will help me sleep. I touch my clitoris. I might not climax; sometimes it's enough to just feel nice. Every so often I decide to sleep naked because I like the feel of the sheets on my skin.

I've got a good imagination. I remember moments. I imagine my ex touching me all over my body, our bodies melting into each other. He scoffed at spirituality, so I know if I had said it to him, he would have thought it ridiculous, but skin on skin, we melted into one another. Once he was very, very tired and I took the initiative. I touched him and aroused him, it was very gentle. He said afterwards,

'Did you help yourself?'

And I had one funny time, we were in bed and the phone rang; it was my mother. She said, 'How are you?' I said, 'Mum, have you ever had to talk to your mother when you're being touched?! I have to hang up.'

Many times I tried to give him up, but it was like a drug because we had so much good sex. Afterwards, I absolutely glowed, and would feel energized and motivated. This man never put me on a pedestal. He never fussed over me. Never bought me gifts. He really didn't do much at all. But I felt incredibly loved. We were together for twenty years.

If he wanted to make love and I had my period, he'd say, 'That's okay, we'll put it off for another day.' I'd deliberately say that so I could hear him say, 'That's okay,' because it was very loving. I was always testing him; this guy was a player. If he said, 'I like your hair like that,' I'd get it changed.

It should have finished much earlier. My conclusion about affairs with married men is that it's a most unhealthy situation, because you can never be spontaneous; you've got to hold your feelings in.

Many women have said, 'I wouldn't do that,' but in my case I had met a lot of men and wasn't attracted

and neither did I. I thought, *I won't get pregnant, it won't happen to me.*

Obviously I got pregnant. I hadn't been feeling well, and my mum said, 'You'll have to do something about this flu, you might have to go to the

I discovered, over the years, that unless I'm emotionally involved, sex won't be enjoyable for me; when I love the person I love the sex.

to anyone. I was alone, not getting any hugs. Never say never, I always say, you don't know, given a certain set of circumstances.

I keep expecting someone to cross my path again. I would be open because I'm still young. But, unless there is a really good connection, I am not interested. I discovered, over the years, that unless I'm emotionally involved, sex won't be enjoyable for me; when I love the person I love the sex.

I enjoy being touched gently and slowly at first. Kisses on my breasts, inner thighs, eyelids, hands stroking my back, fingers through my hair. I even enjoy fast, no-mucking-around sex as long as the mood is right and the attraction is strong, otherwise it feels like you are being attacked.

I started out completely ignorant. My future husband and I started having sex when I was about eighteen. Neither of us had ever slept with anyone before and we wanted to see what it was like. He had no knowledge

doctor.' It was my sister who said, 'She's pregnant!' I thought, *Oh my God, I didn't even know myself.* My mother looked at me. 'Didn't you use anything?' This has stuck in my mind. I was really angry at her, not that I expressed it. *Man, they tell you nothing and you're supposed to know all about it!*

We were married for thirteen years, until I found out about his affairs. When we divorced, I was only hit on by married men. Welcome to the world.

Alice Skinner is a London-based illustrator and visual artist. She creates tongue-in-cheek and digestible images as a social commentary on 21st-century life. ◙ @thisisaliceskinner

ILLUSTRATION BY ALICE SKINNER

Running Press
Hachette Book Group
1290 Avenue of the Americas, New York, NY 10104
www.runningpress.com
@Running_Press

Printed in China

Published by Running Press, an imprint of Perseus Books, LLC, a subsidiary of Hachette Book Group, Inc.

Illustrations: p.7 Natalie Krim; p.11 @MariNaomi; pp. 15, 63, 93,157,215 © Barbara Malagoli; pp. 19, 149 © Arnelle Woker; pp. 23, 179 © Nikki Peck; p.27 © Candie Payne; pp. 33, 197 © Anshika Khullar; pp. 37, 189 © Kate Philipson; pp. 41, 145, 223 © Alice Skinner; pp. 45, 75 © Regards Coupables; p. 49 © Elsa Rose Frere; pp. 53, 119, 167, 201 © Sabrina Gevaerd; p. 59 © Mattia Cavanna; p. 67 © Tina Maria Elena; pp. 71, 141 © Kim Thompson; p. 79 © Rachel Gadsden; p. 85 © Sofie Birkin; pp. 89, 123,175 © Jasmine Chin; p. 97 © Jemima Williams; pp. 101, 153 © Alphachanneling; p. 105 © 2021 KaCeyKal!; p.111 © Naomi Vona; p. 115 © Emily Marcus; p. 127 © Chrissie Hynde; p. 131 © Ojima Abalaka; pp. 137, 183 © Destiny Darcel; p. 163 © Sarah B. Whalen; pp. 171, 209 © Frances Cannon; p. 193 © Golden Daze Illustration; p. 205 © Miranda Lorikeet; p. 219 © Jenny Eclair

Cover illustration by Bárbara Malagoli
Design by Sarah Greeno

Library of Congress Control Number: 2020951565

ISBNs: 978-0-7624-7448-6 (hardcover), 978-0-7624-7447-9 (ebook)

1010

10 9 8 7 6 5 4 3 2 1

If you need help or simply more information, please consider getting in touch with the following charities:

Galop supports LGBT+ victims and survivors of sexual abuse, domestic violence and hate crime.
www.galop.org.uk

Refuge provides specialist support for women and children experiencing domestic violence.
www.nationaldahelpline.org.uk

Stonewall is committed to empowering all LGBTT people to be their authentic selves.
www.stonewall.org.uk

The Dahlia Project wants to achieve an end to Female Genital Mutlation (FGM) by creating safe spaces to support individuals and societies affected by FGM.
www.dahliaproject.org

Brook is committed to changing attitudes, challenging prejudices and championing equality so that all young people can lead happy, healthy lives
www.brook.org.uk